HOW TO VISIT A MUSEUM

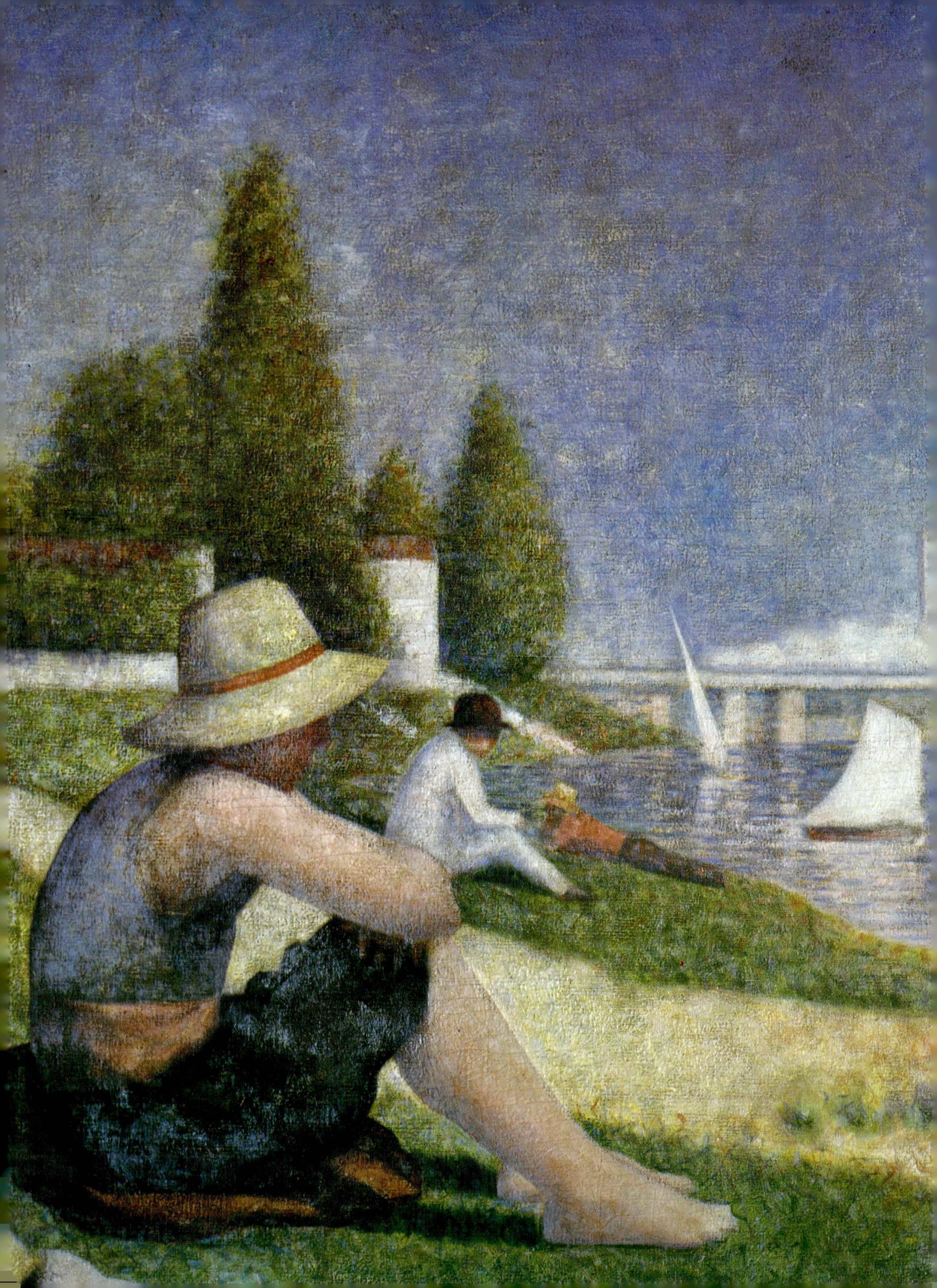

HOW TO VISIT A MUSEUM

By David Finn

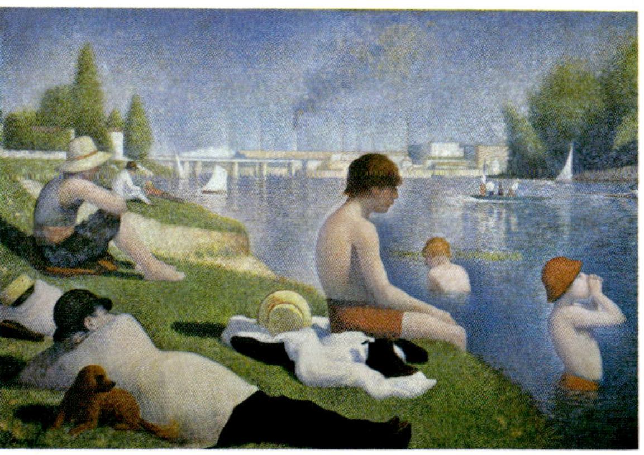

Harry N. Abrams, Inc. Publishers, New York

Project Director: Margaret L. Kaplan
Designer: Ulrich Ruchti and
Michael Schubert, Associate Designer.

Library of Congress Cataloging in Publication Data
Finn, David, 1921–
How to visit a museum.
1. Art museums. 2. Art appreciation. I. Title.
N410.F56 1985 708 84-14461
ISBN 0-8109-2297-5

Published in 1985 by Harry N. Abrams, Incorporated, New York. Printed and bound in Japan.

CONTENTS

PREFACE

In the spring of 1979, Henry Moore told me of an idea he had to publish a book on what the British Museum had meant to him during his formative years as a sculptor. He wanted to identify those sculptures that had made a deep impression on him and explain why. He thought it might help others to find their own favorite works in this great collection and to discover how meaningful museum visits can be to a creative person.

Since I had become a specialist in photographing sculpture and had published over a dozen books aimed at revealing the inner qualities of three-dimensional works of art, Henry Moore wondered if I would be interested in working with him on the project, and photographing the sculptures that he wanted to describe. I was fascinated by the idea, and two years later the book, *Henry Moore at the British Museum,* was published. It proved to be one of his and my favorite projects.

Subsequently, Michael Hoare, managing director of the British Museum Publishing Company, suggested that I consider building on this basic idea and creating a book on *How to Visit a Museum.* I had visited literally hundreds of museums around the world both as a tourist and as a photographer working on various books, and the idea seemed intriguing. But is was not until Paul Gottlieb and Margaret Kaplan of Harry N. Abrams, Inc., suggested that I write an informal and rather personal text on my own feelings about museum-going that this book was born.

While working on the text, I mentioned the theme to many of my friends, who startled me with their eagerness to learn whatever they could about how to get more out of their museum visits. It seems that the uncertainty of what to do when one has passed through the portals of a museum is almost universal. My goal has been to present some thoughts on the subject that might help readers feel more confident in themselves and more open to rewarding experiences on future museum visits.

The illustrations are largely chosen from my own photographic files. These are pictures I have made for my own enjoyment of the works, very much as I have recommended to others in the text. There are a substantial number of photographs of sculpture, since my camera eye tends to be drawn to those works. Photographs of details of paintings are usually mine as well. Some of the full-scale reproductions of paintings were obtained directly from museums.

I make no claim that the works pictured or described in this book are in any way a representative selection of great works of art in the museums of the world. I have included, for the most part, references to those works that help to make a particular point and also that happened to be among my favorites. In that I have followed a principle described by W. B. Yeats, who wrote in the introduction to a volume of selections from Spenser:

> I have not tried to select what people call characteristic passages, for that is, I think, the way to make a dull book. One never really knows anybody's taste but one's own, and if one likes any-

thing sincerely one may be certain that there are other people made out of the same earth to like it too.

I believe that all museum-goers should develop their own storehouse of memories and impressions in the course of their lives. This can create in each of us a unique amalgam of esthetic experiences that will enrich our lives. My hope is that readers of this book will be helped to do so by seeing how this particular museum-goer has benefited in the course of developing his own experiences.

WHAT TO LOOK FOR

There is no right or wrong way to visit a museum. The most important rule you should keep in mind as you go through the front door is to follow your own instincts. Be prepared to find what excites you, to enjoy what delights your heart and mind, perhaps to have esthetic experiences you will never forget. You have a feast in store for you and you should make the most of it. Stay as long or as short a time as you will, but do your best at all times to let the work of art speak directly to you with a minimum of interference or distraction.

The first moment you walk into a museum is filled with excitement and expectation. You may be so anxious to get started that you overlook the map posted at the entranceway or printed in a folder available at the front desk. However, taking a minute or two to get an overview of what is in the museum could save you the frustration of missing a part of the collection you would particularly enjoy—like the extraordinary "black paintings" by Goya, which many visitors to the Prado in Madrid do not realize are hung in the basement galleries. If you want to prepare yourself more thoroughly, spend some time before you start through the galleries studying the official museum guidebook or a general one such as the Blue Guide, which offers a room-by-room description of the works on display. When I have

Francisco Goya
The Witches' Sabbath
(detail).
1821–22.
Oil on canvas,
4′7⅛″ x 14′4½″.
The Prado Museum, Madrid

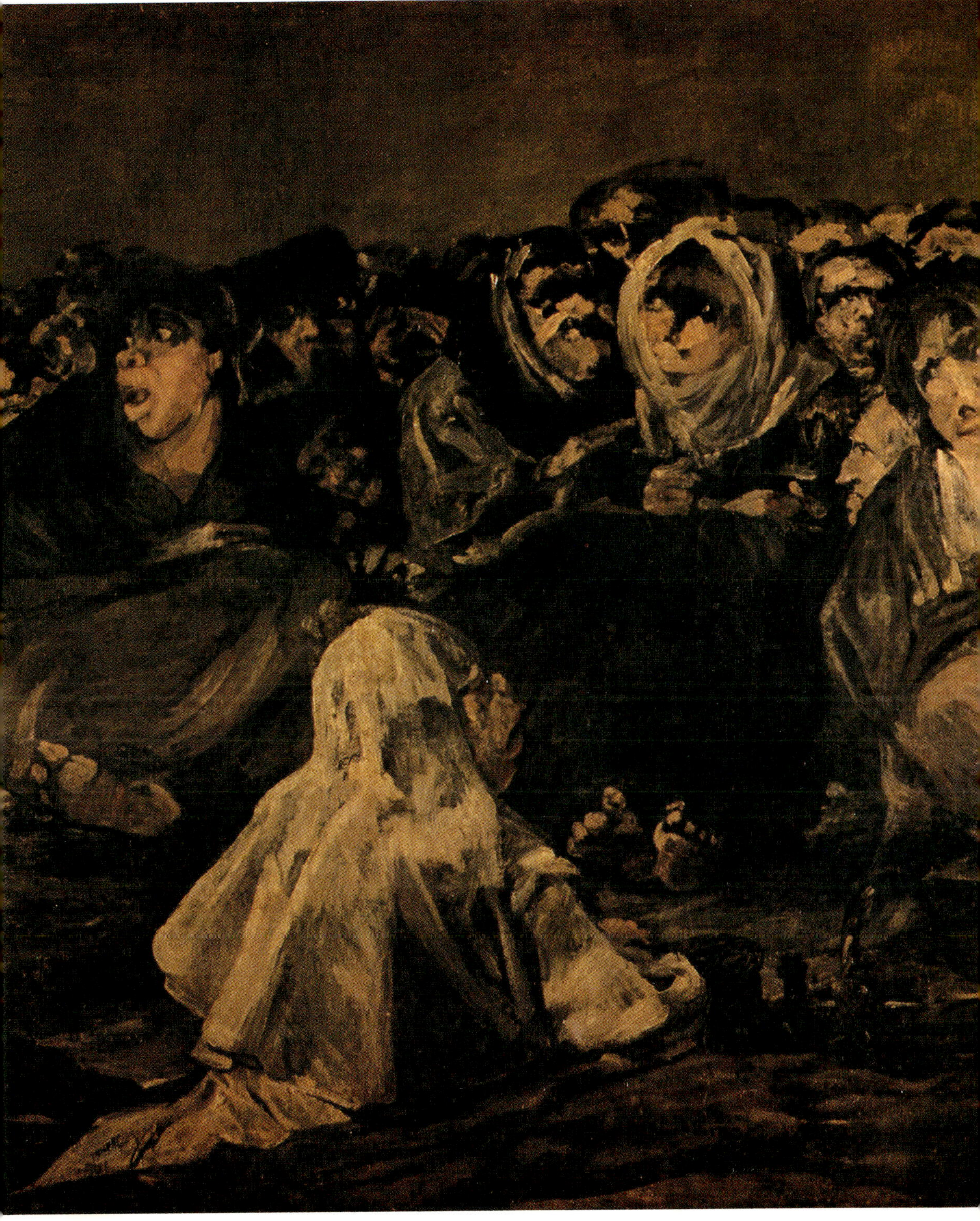

taken the time to do so, underlining the works I want to be sure to see, it has been rewarding. Not that I always hunt for those particular works when I get to the museum—that could be too distracting. But just knowing what kinds of works to expect somehow helps put me in the right frame of mind for the visit.

The Egyptian Gallery in the British Museum, London

No matter how much or little preparation you have done, however, you cannot help being stunned when the first major gallery turns out to be an enormous room filled with extraordinary works of art. Take, for example, the Egyptian Gallery at the British Museum, which must include a hundred large and small objects. Where and how to begin? The giant roaring Assyrian lion at the entranceway seems almost part of the architecture, so you may ignore it unless you look carefully at its fantastic head and mouth and sense its enormous strength. Nearby is the famous Rosetta Stone, its label explaining that it was this fragment of black basalt that enabled archaeologists to unravel the mystery of hieroglyphics. There is a thrill in standing before an object that played such an important role in deciphering the past.

But what about the rest of the Egyptian Gallery? Do you look at one object after another, noting how large some of the monumental figures are, how curious the animal forms seem to be, how remarkable it is that the figures were so realistic thousands of years ago? Should you make a point of examining them all? How much time should you spend in the little side rooms off the main gallery where some especially important objects may be on display? What should you *think about* as you look at the objects? How beautiful they are? How historically significant? How being near them brings you closer to an ancient civilization?

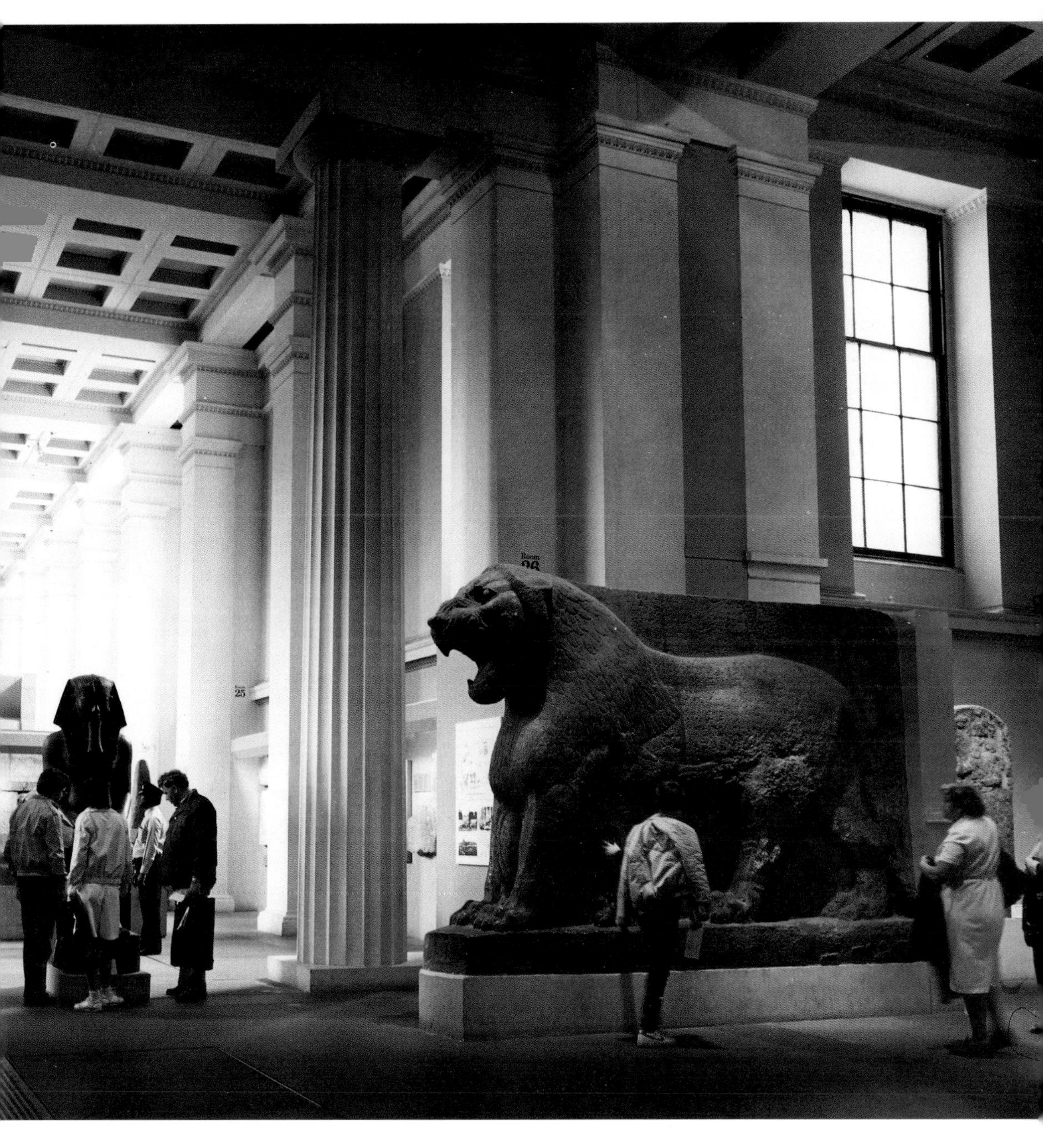
Room
26
Room
25

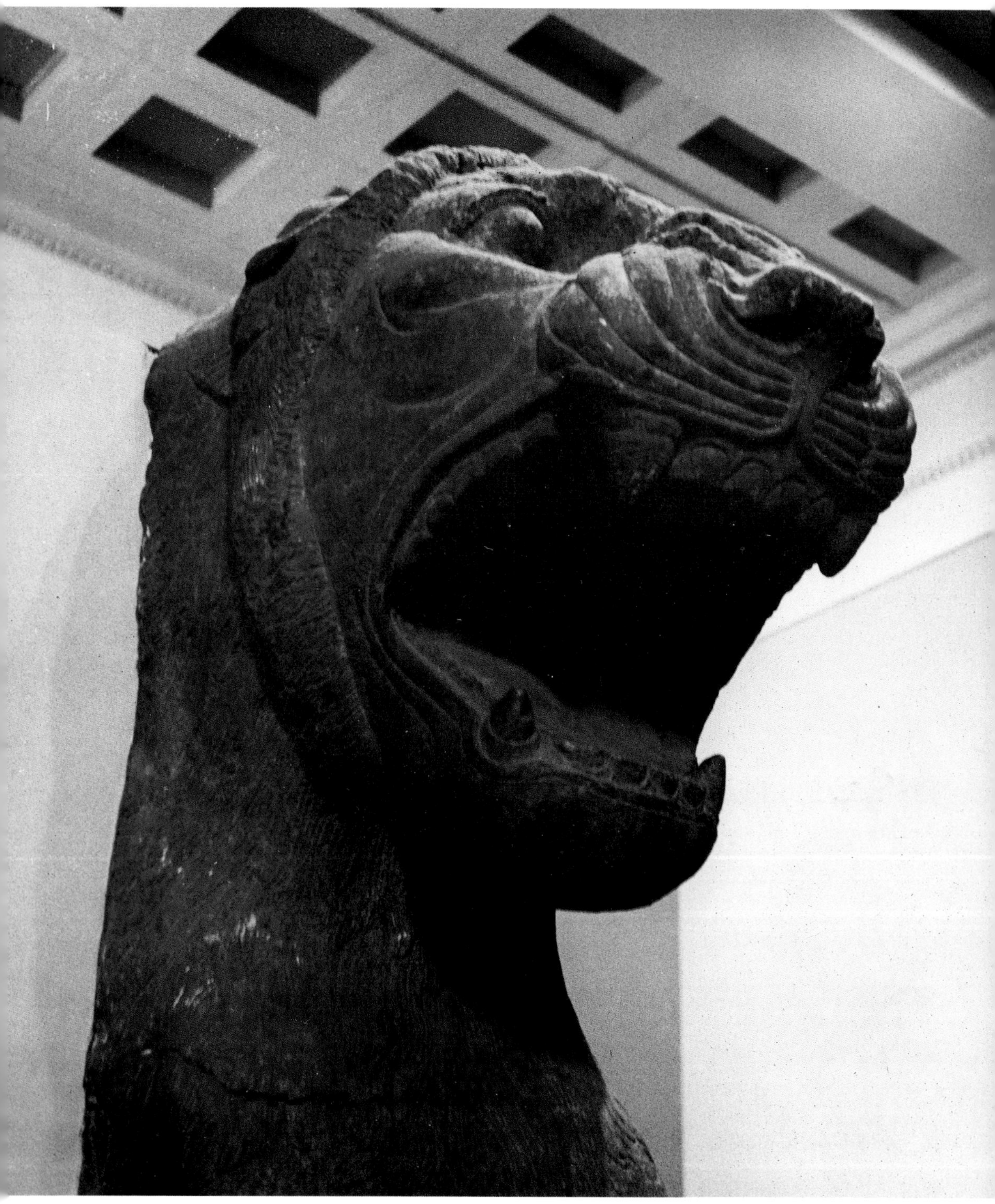

Opposite:
Assyrian Lion (detail)
Late Assyrian,
9th century B.C.
Limestone, height of head about 3′.
British Museum, London

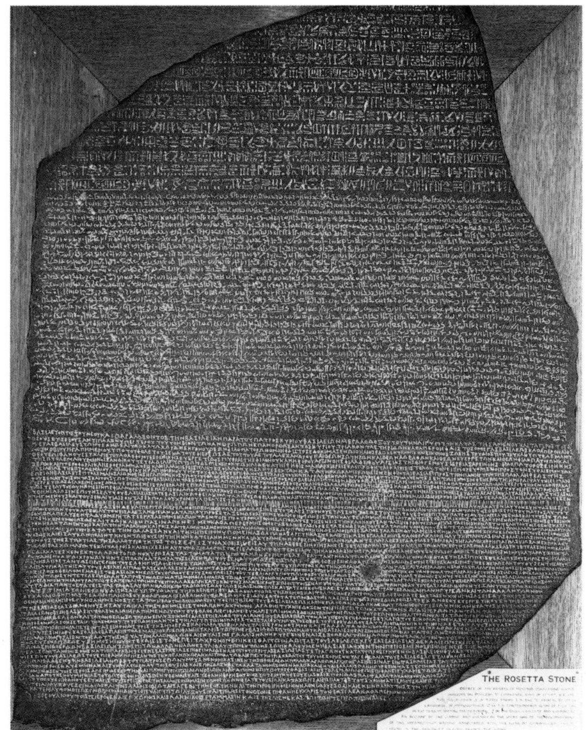

Rosetta Stone
c. 196 B.C.
Basalt fragment.
British Museum, London

Any one of these or a thousand other thoughts may go through your mind. You may wonder about the identity of the royal personage portrayed in a monumental head mounted on a tall pedestal, and be impressed by the giant arm mounted below, which appears to be another fragment of the same sculpture. If you look at both casually, you will probably see only a curious remnant from another civilization, where people wore strange headdresses and created enormous monuments. But if you look at the features of the face more closely you will find a wonderfully sensitive portrait of a handsome young man who may even remind you of someone you know. And if you walk around the clenched fist, you will discover a

Overleaf:
Head of Amenophis III
c. 1400 B.C. Red granite.
Arm of Amenophis II.
British Museum, London

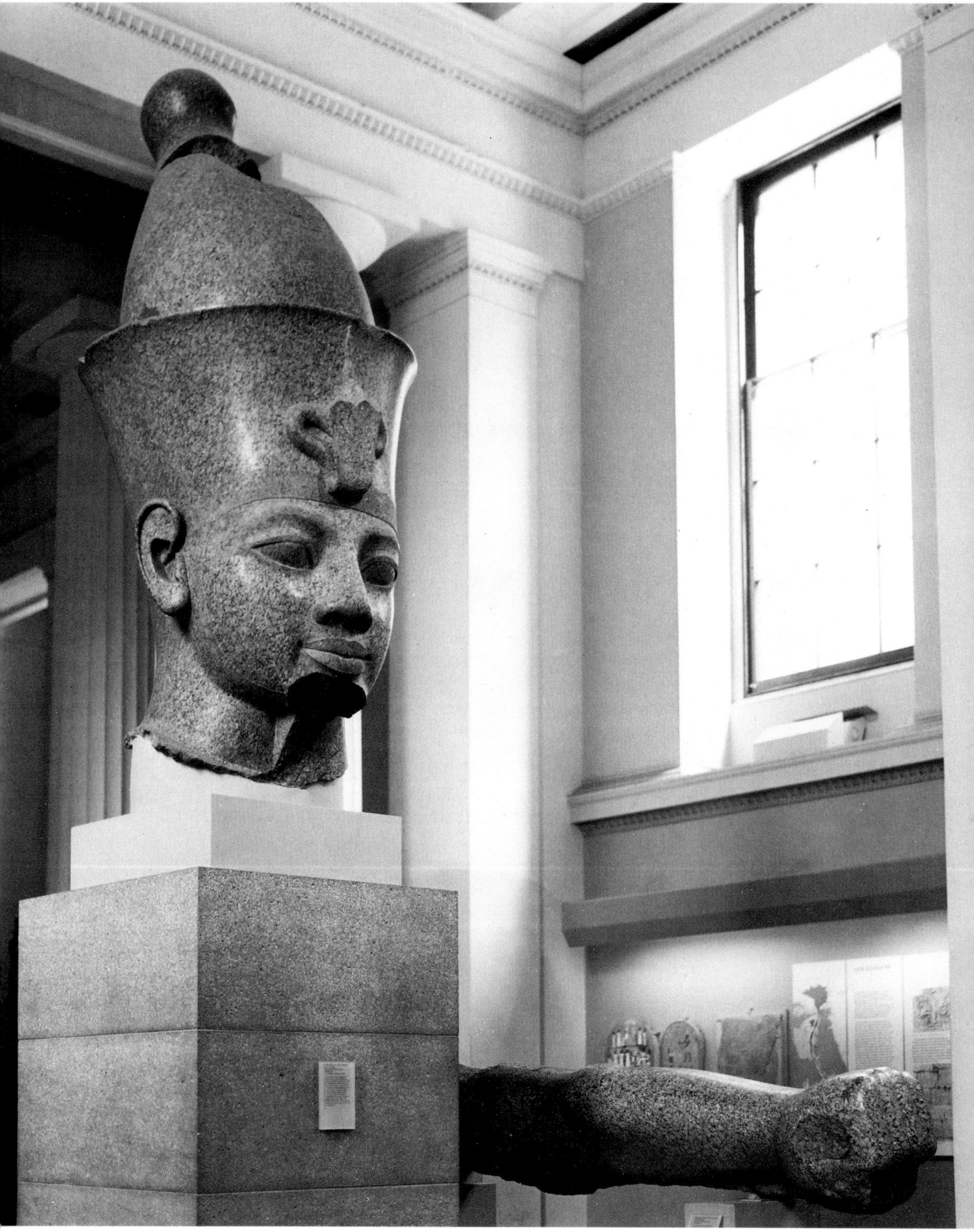

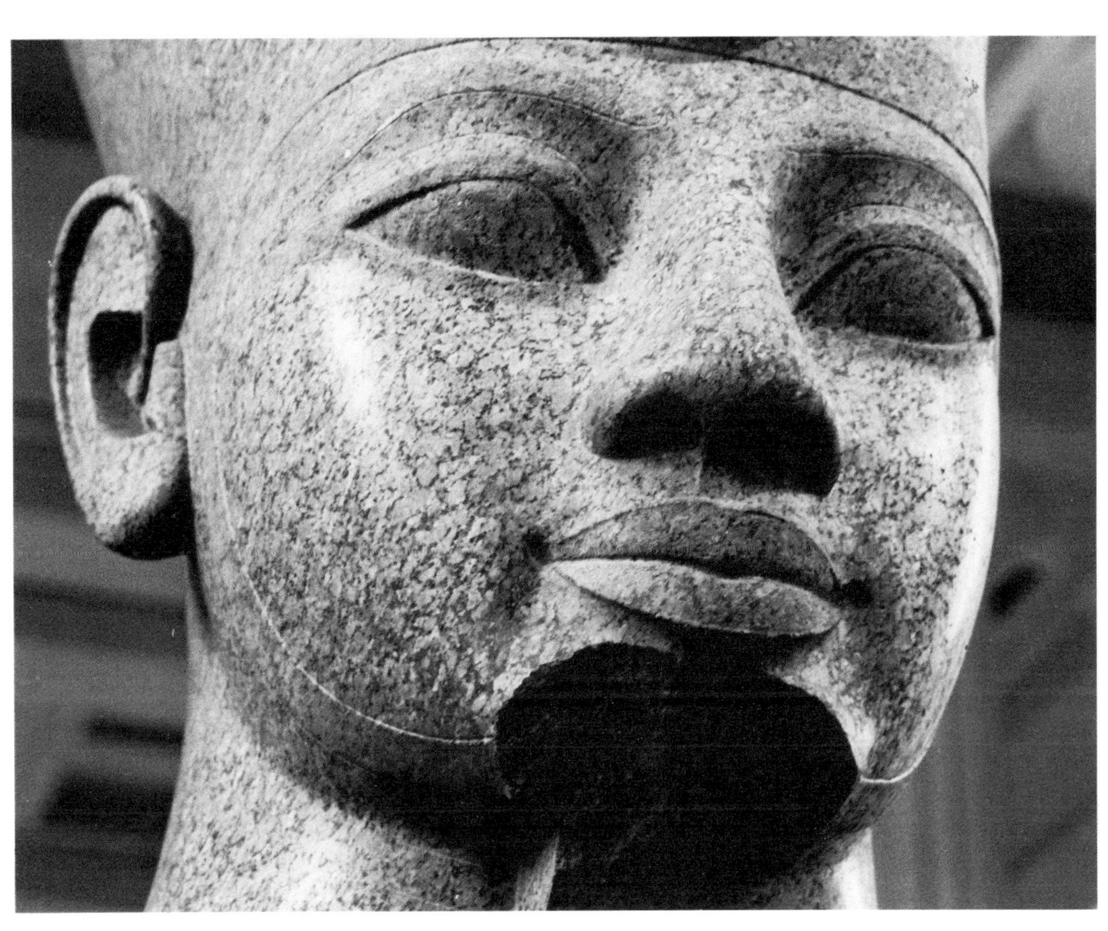

symphony of form that is a sculptural tour de force in its own right.

What was there about that era and the attitude people had toward their godlike rulers, you may ask yourself, that produced these overpowering images? And what should our attitude be toward them today? Once I visited the Egyptian Gallery with a renowned theologian and asked why these figures, which seem like such great sculptures to our eyes, were condemned in the Old Testament as idols. "It's one thing to appreciate the figures as art," he replied, "but quite another to worship them." I tried vainly to look at the images as the ancient Egyptians or Israelites must have seen them and had an eerie sense of the changes wrought over millenniums, bridged in a remarkable way by the universality of artistic expression that dazzled my eyes.

DEVELOPING YOUR OWN PACE. Most of the problems you are likely to find in walking through a museum come from within yourself. You may worry about paying too little attention to the most important paintings and sculptures in the collection. When you recognize the name of a well-known artist, you may be excited by what you see but wonder if it is his reputation or his work that impresses you. You also may worry because you are ignoring works by artists you do not happen to know. You are anxious not to miss anything as you wander through the galleries, but at the same time you know you cannot do justice to *everything* in the museum.

It is natural to want to look at least once at everything on your initial visit to any museum. This is certainly true if the museum is in a distant city and you do not know when you will have a chance to visit it again. It is hard to curb this tendency, and most often you just have to give in to it, hoping that some vivid memory of greatness will stand out from the blur. Too often one thinks that going to a museum is like reading a book; if one does not read every page all the way through to the end, one is not doing right by the author. It takes some courage to stop reading a book in the middle, and one only does so if the author totally fails to excite one's interest. A museum is just the opposite. The problem is how not to become surfeited.

There is a distinct, almost measurable response curve in visiting a museum, with those objects you see at the outset making a greater impact than those you see later on. The rate of diminishing response varies from individual to individual and may also vary from museum to museum. The climax of your visit could come at any point along the way, but the bleary-eyed phenomenon is inevitable, and you definitely will be able to absorb less of what you see as time goes on. There is nothing you can do about this, so do not worry about it. If you want to be sure at least to *see* everything even though you no longer *feel* anything, walk through the rest of the museum quickly. It will give you an overview of what is there. But you may prefer to quit when your capacity to react has worn out, for it can be a great trial to walk through gallery after gallery after you have become numb to what you are seeing.

Remember you are not going to take a quiz at the end of your visit, so you do not have to account for all the objects in the museum. If you can leave the museum with a sense of having seen some magnificent works and with a few images indelibly imprinted

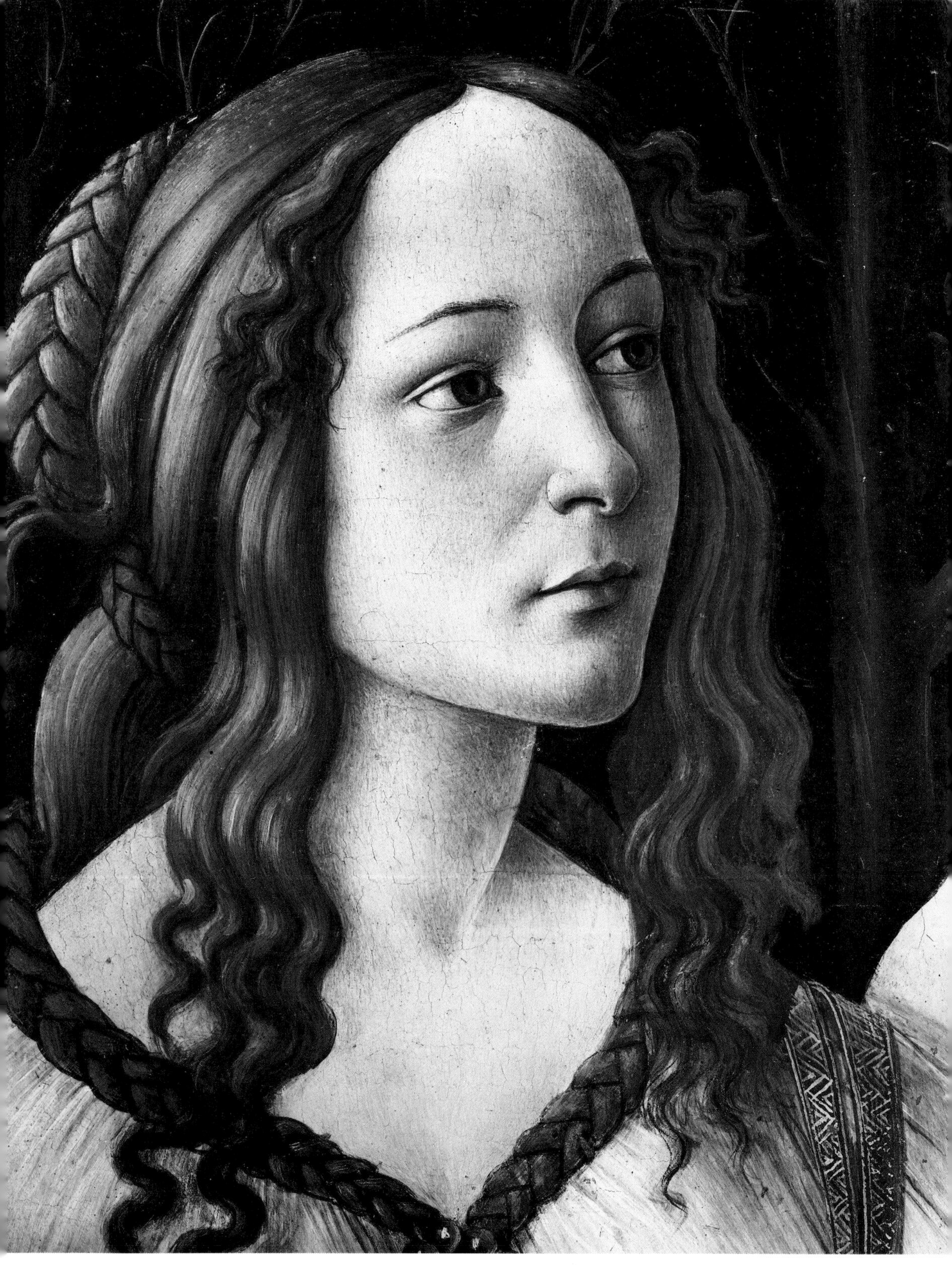

Sandro Botticelli
Venus and Mars (detail).
c. 1475.
Panel, 27¼ x 68¼″.
National Gallery, London

in your brain, even if you cannot remember where they came from or even who the artists were, your visit will have been a success.

Some people give themselves an arbitrary one-hour limit for any museum visit. Some can go two hours without running into trouble, but others tire after a half-hour. I find that the length of time I can spend in a museum varies, depending on where I am, what I am seeing, what my mood is, and probably many other unidentifiable influences. But I know there is always *some* limit to my endurance.

Often it is possible to take a break and relax for a few minutes on a couch in one of the galleries. Seating areas are designed for your convenience, and if you feel your feet wearing out or your mind filling up with too many images, a change of pace can do a lot of good. This is particularly rewarding if you sit in front of a work of art that you would enjoy looking at in some detail.

An even longer break for a cup of coffee or lunch in the cafeteria can be especially useful if you are in a large museum and want to visit a new section or special exhibition with a fresh mind.

WHERE TO BEGIN. I still remember my first trip to the National Gallery of Art in London. My adventure began, as it does with most visitors, by turning to the left of the entranceway, walking into medieval galleries, and following through chronologically to the rest of the museum collection. The paintings in the early galleries were revelations, and I was enormously excited to see works by Piero della Francesca, Botticelli, and others I had long known through reproductions. Looking closely at the details

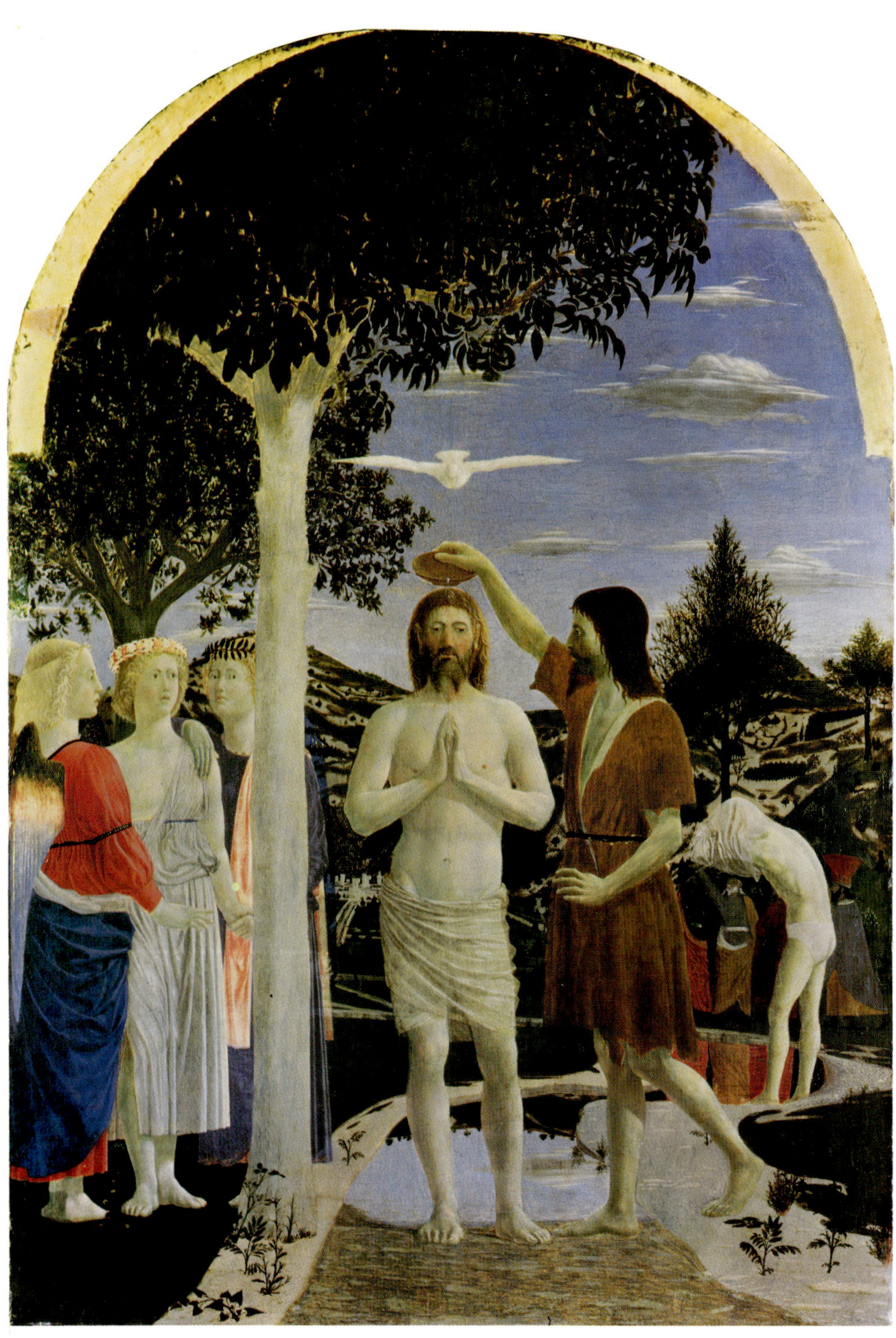

Piero della Francesca
Baptism of Christ. c. 1450.
Panel, 66 x 45¾".
National Gallery, London

Below: Detail

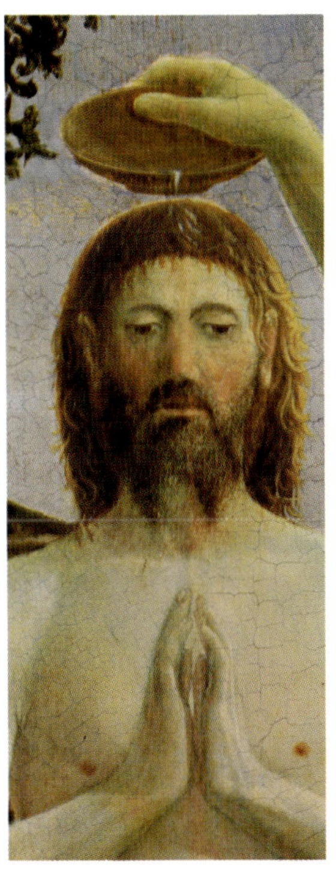

of these paintings was extraordinary. It was not only marvelous to be able to see them "in the flesh," but also to explore various sections of the canvases and discover how the figures were rendered so beautifully. My faculties held up through a dozen or so galleries—past the Raphaels, Michelangelos, Correggios, Veroneses, Titians, and so on. Then, when I reached the Rembrandts, I had to push myself to see what was there. Afterward I started walking faster because I simply could not focus my eyes any more. I glanced through succeeding rooms, recognizing Velázquez, Goya, Murillo—but not having enough esthetic energy left to stand in front of each for more than a few seconds. By the time I came to the last few galleries I was an empty shell. Nothing had any meaning for me other than a passing, almost grudging acknowledgment of who painted what.

It was not until some years later, during my third or fourth visit to the museum, that I got the idea of walking through the museum in the opposite direction. It took an enormous wrench not to begin at the beginning, but instead of going to the left, I went to the right. And there, ablaze in an explosion of light, was a magnificent collection of French Impressionist paintings I had never been able to enjoy in the past. There was that magnificent Seurat *Bathing at Asnières* that absolutely dazzles the eye, several spellbinding Van Goghs, and some of the most monumental Cézannes I had ever seen. Farther on I found a room full of Ingres paintings that I had never looked at closely before. And, like a special gift, a beautiful bust portrait called *The Surprise* by a painter named Claude-Marie Dubufe, whom I had never heard of before. It was as if I were seeing that part of the museum for the first time. I appreciated the last galleries of the museum as if I had never been there on any previous visit.

Curators have all sorts of reasons for arranging works of art in a particular order. History is usually a major factor in their thinking. Also, schools of art and geographical regions tend to be grouped together. In a large museum, curatorial departments control separate galleries—Primitive, Egyptian, Greek and Roman, Medieval, Renaissance, etc. But visitors do not have to be prisoners of these arrangements. You can think of yourself as a wanderer in unexplored territory. Often the best way is just to plunge in and start looking, moving from room to room without worrying about sequence.

Georges Seurat
Bathing at Asnières.
1883–84 (retouched 1887).
Oil on canvas,
6′7″ x 9′10½″.
National Gallery, London

Opposite: Detail

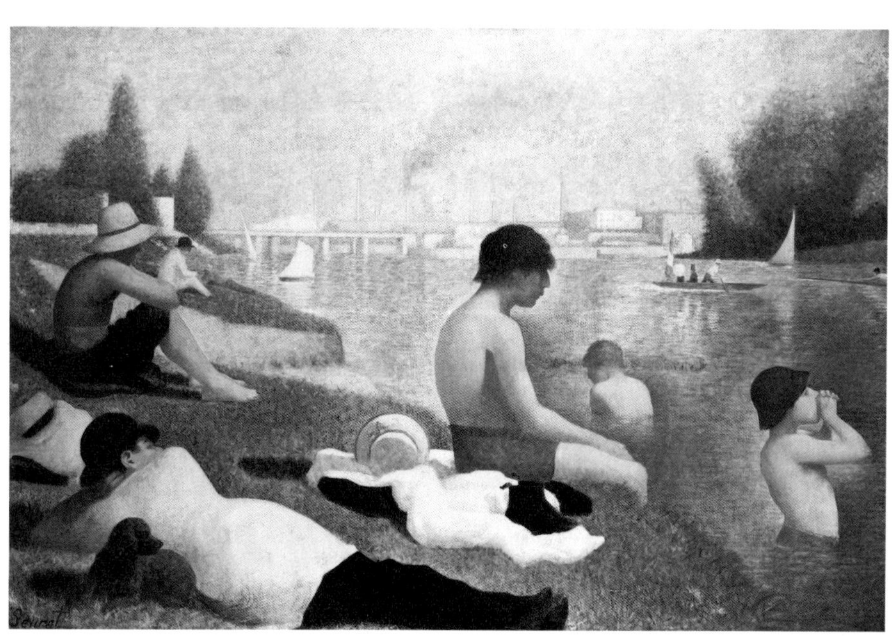

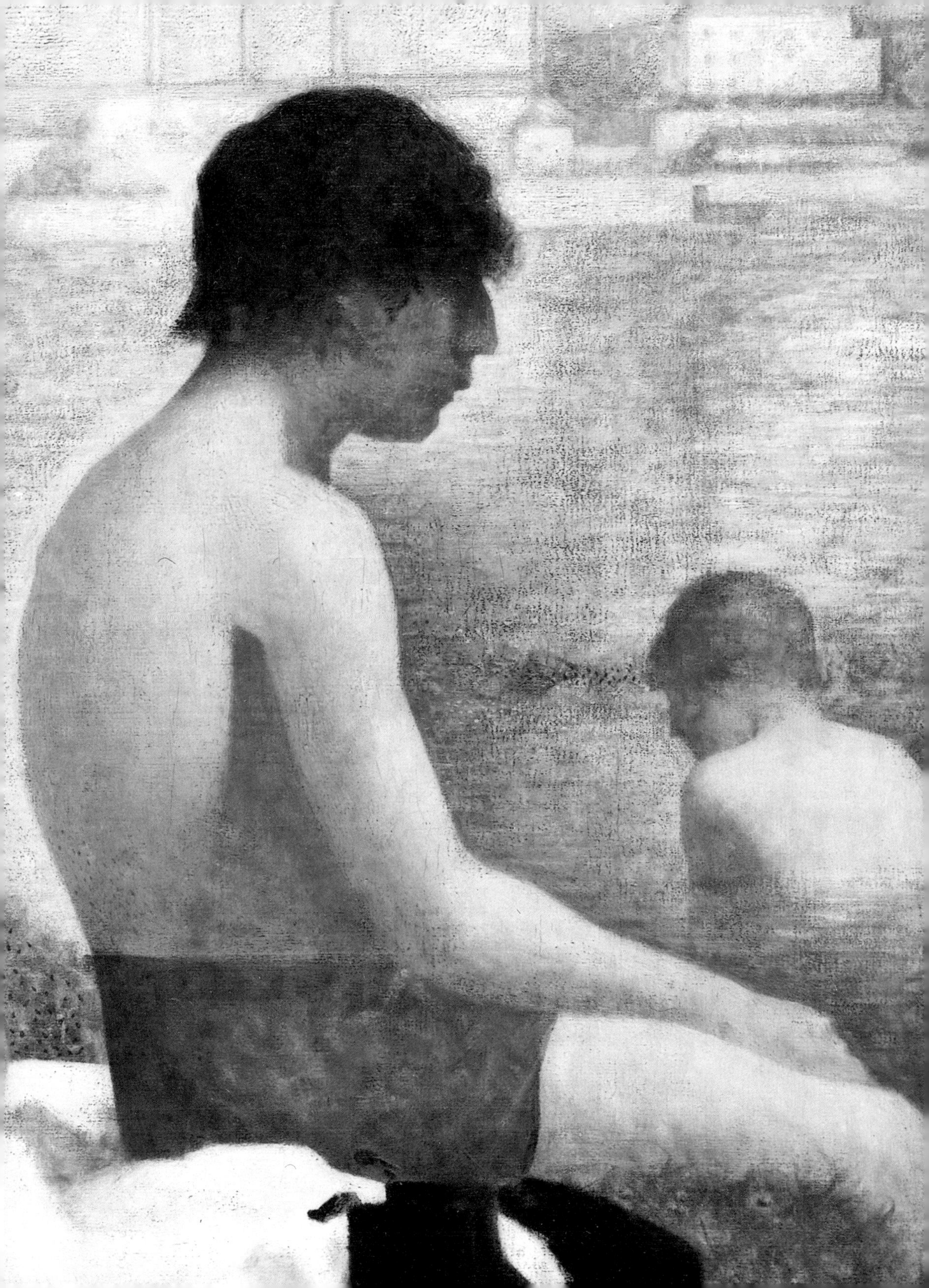

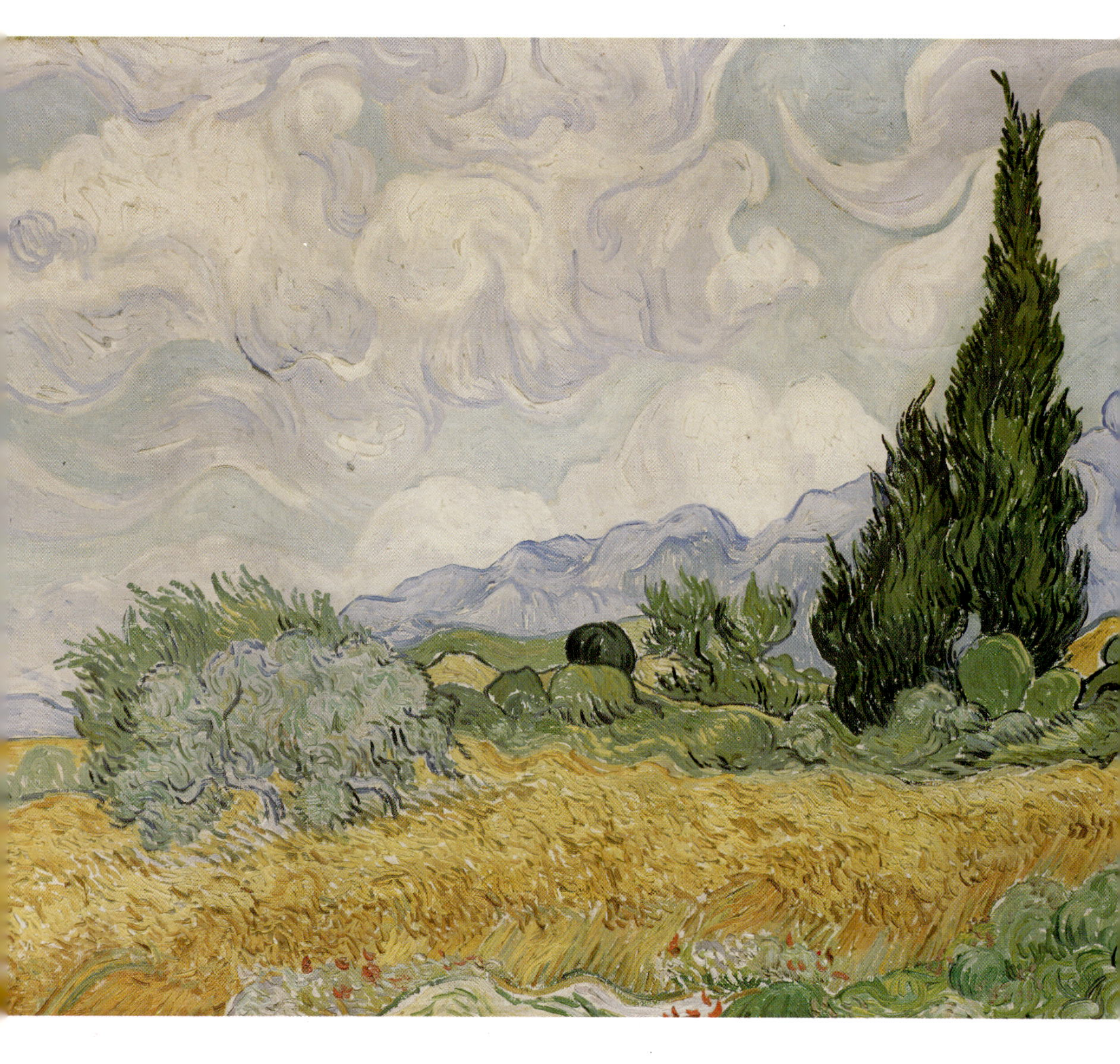

Vincent van Gogh
Wheatfield with Cypresses.
1889.
Oil on canvas, 28½ x 36″.
National Gallery, London

DISPLAYS CAN DRAMATIZE—BUT DON'T LET THEM FOOL YOU. In most museums today, considerable care is taken in how works of art are displayed, and there is no doubt that the manner of display will influence your reaction. When the exhibition "The Vatican Collections" opened at the Metropolitan Museum in New York, one of the largest galleries featured three objects—the *Apollo Belvedere,* the *Belvedere Torso,* and a Raphael tapestry. One *had* to look at each with a sense of awe; the space around it was part of the experience. In their original locations in the Vatican, they were never in the same kind of spotlight. The *Apollo* was one of a dozen or so sculptures placed in the Belvedere court, and the *Torso* stood in the midst of what seemed to be a jumble of other works. Looking at them in the Metropolitan exhibition was a new experience. Suddenly one noticed details that were absolutely breathtaking. It was incredible to see the beautifully composed folds under Apollo's outstretched arm, the details of the sandals on his feet, and the majestic view of the upper torso, all of which would have been difficult to view in his previous, relatively cramped quarters.

Still, there is an art to being able to pick out an object in a crowded area and discovering how spectacularly beautiful it is. This requires concentrated examination of each object. Henry Moore remembers the British Museum when its galleries consisted of one jam-packed display case after another. As a young sculptor he visited the museum regularly, and discovered marvelous works of art that he identified with his own searching eye. There is a special excite-

Overleaf:
Apollo Belvedere
Roman copy, c. 130–40, after a Greek bronze original, c. 330 B.C., attributed to Leochares.
Parian marble, height 88¼″.
The Vatican, Rome

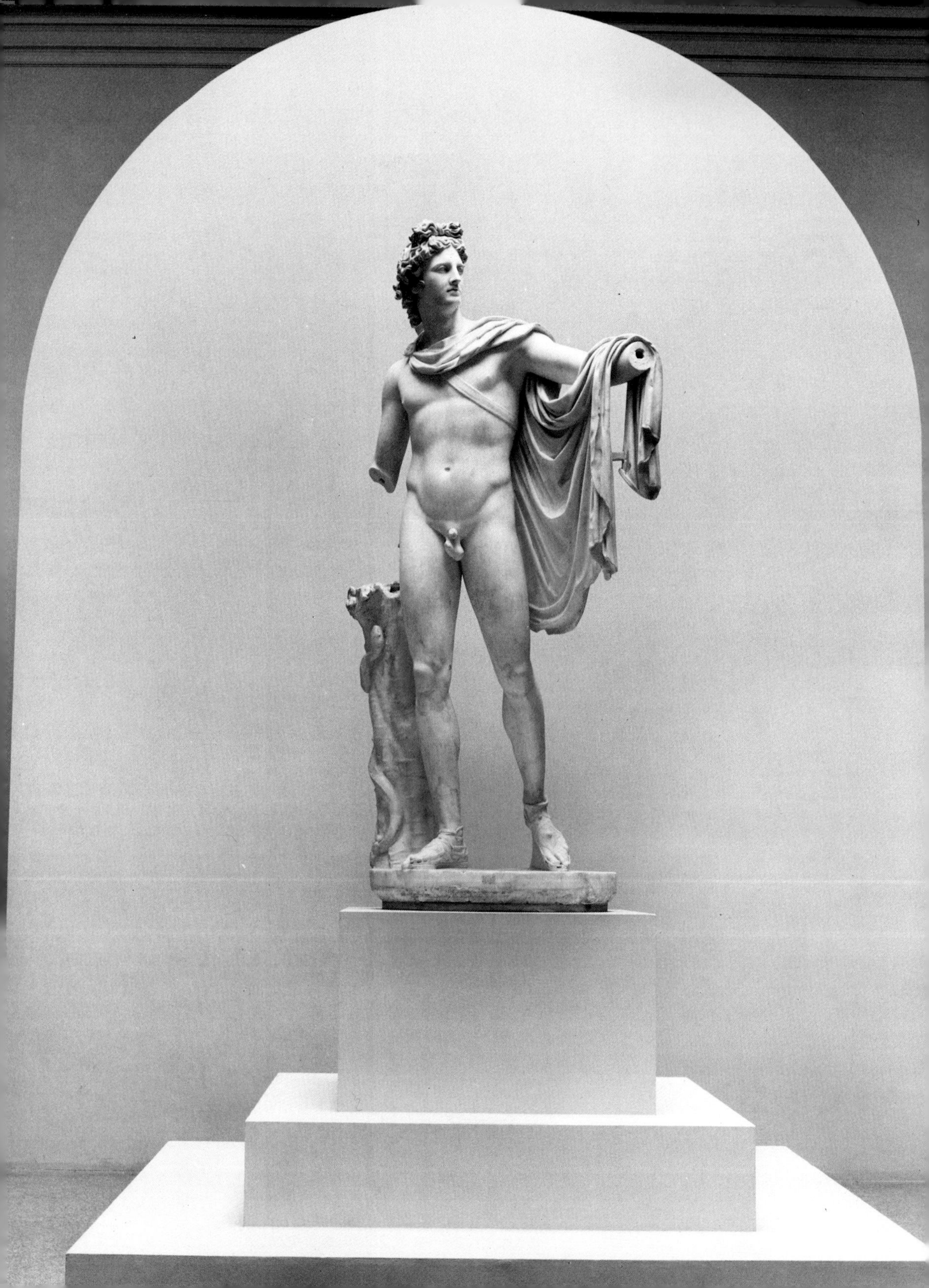

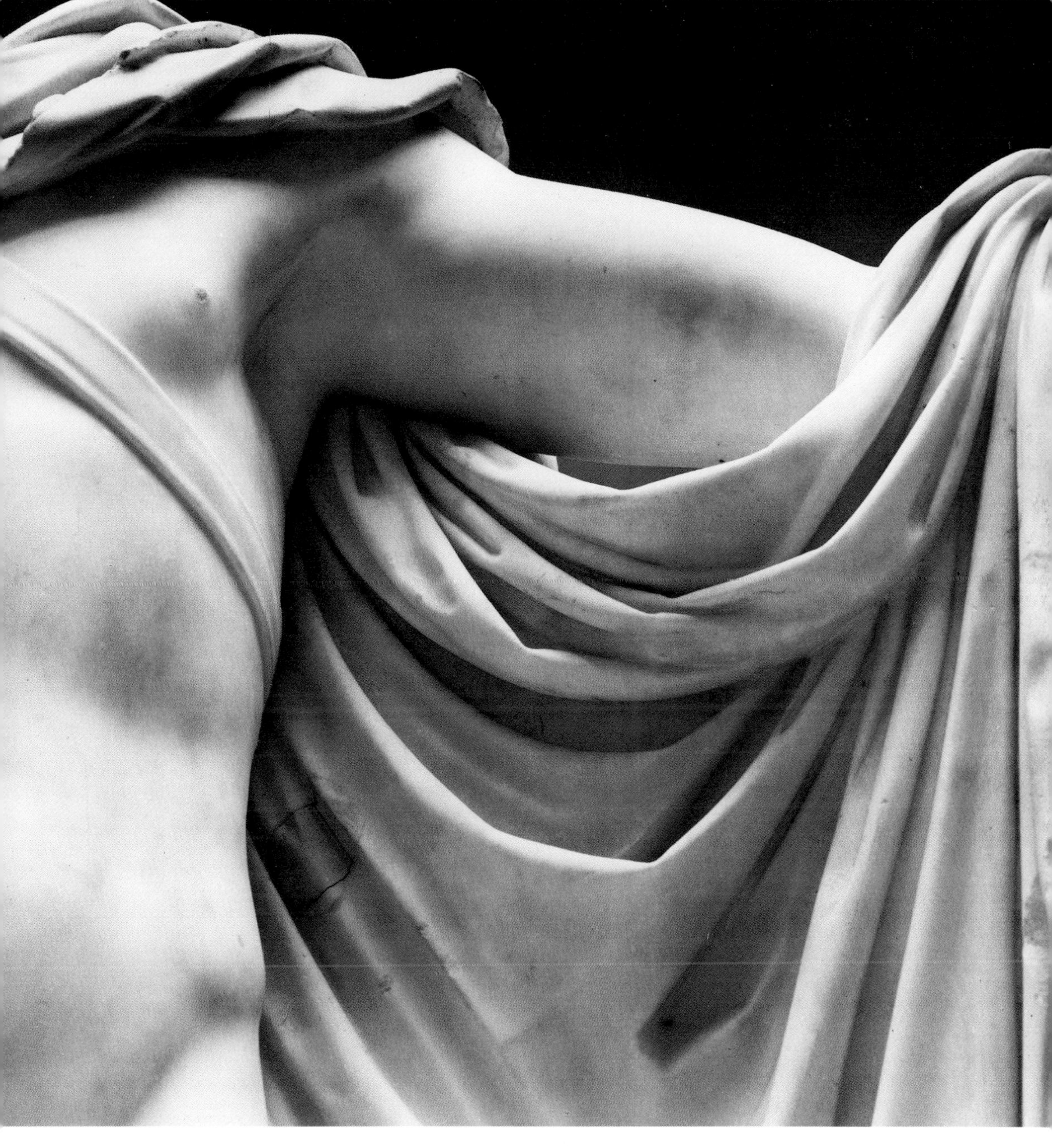

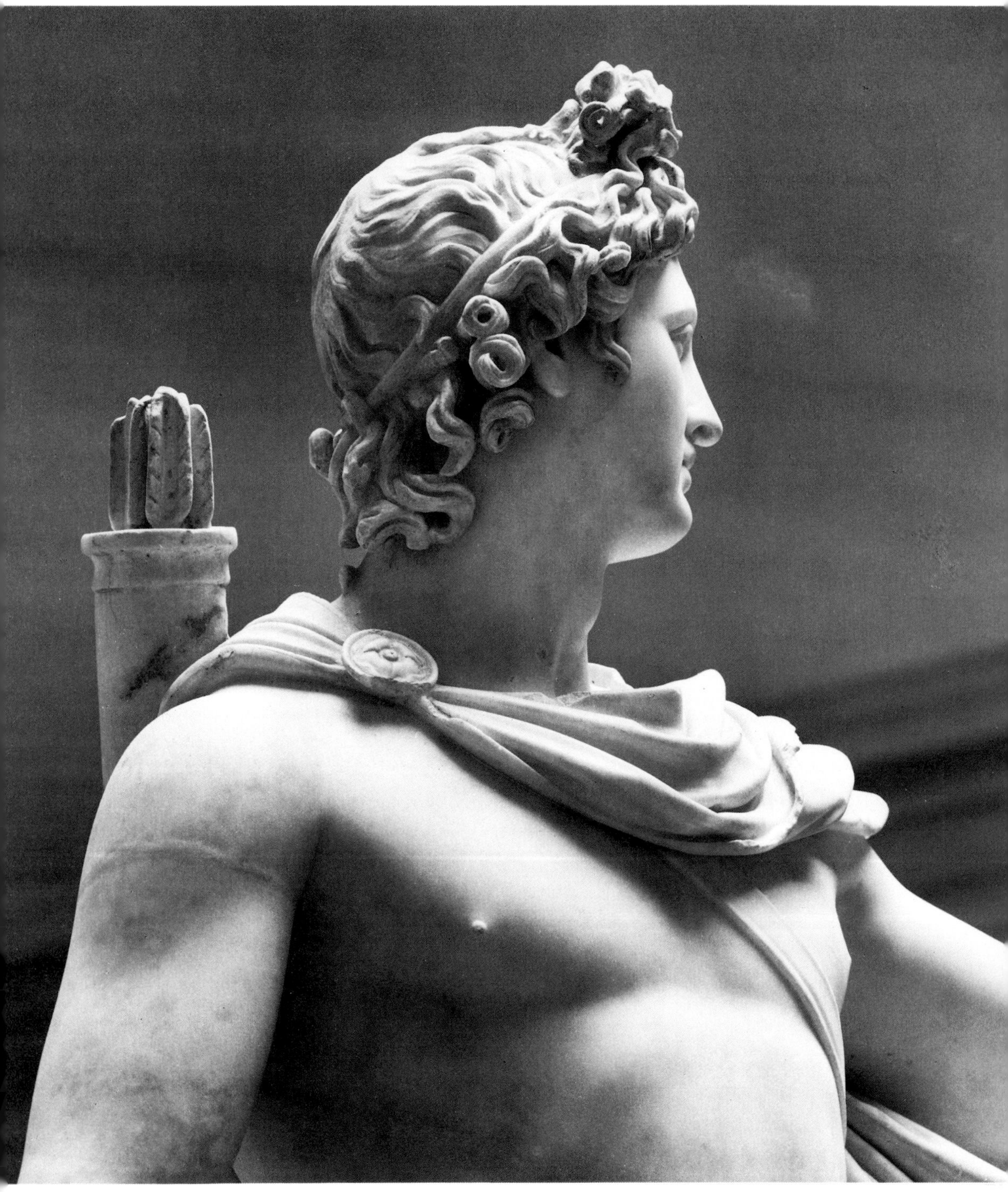

Detail of *Apollo Belvedere*

ment when you find masterpieces on your own.

Looking at sculpture carefully is a problem in many museums where paintings seem to be the prime objects on display. The sculptural works may be placed almost as decoration in galleries, and you have to remind yourself that they are as worthy of esthetic attention as the spotlighted paintings. The almost universal museum rule not to touch sculpture is very frustrating because great sculpture cries out to be felt. The rubbed bronze of particularly appetizing anatomical parts suggests that at least in some instances visitors manage to have their way.

There can also be a sort of "emperor's clothes" phenomenon in which one imagines there are wonderful qualities in a work of art that is prominently displayed. At the Accademia in Florence, the *Palestrina Pietà* has long been presented as if it were one of Michelangelo's great works. Visitors move past the *St. Matthew* and the four *Slaves* located on both sides of the gallery, reaching the *Pietà* just before coming into the large gallery with the *David*. There is a sort of crescendo moving from the powerful *Slaves* to the dramatic *Pietà* to the awesome *David*. So universal was the acclaim for the *Palestrina Pietà* that when John Pope-Hennessy wrote an essay stating that it could not possibly be by Michelangelo, even scholars found it hard to believe. Yet if one visits the Accademia today, after knowing why Pope-Hennessy came to his conclusion, it is easy to see that the *Palestrina Pietà* does not deserve its prominent position. It is ungainly from most points of view; the chisel marks in the sculpture are clumsy; and the anatomy of the body is so badly articulated that the attribution could not possibly be correct. It is hard to remember believing this work to be by Michelangelo.

THERE'S NO RULE ON HOW LONG IT TAKES TO APPRECIATE A MASTERPIECE. As you move around the gallery you may wonder how much time it takes to absorb the qualities of a major work of art. The answer has to be that the depth of appreciation is not a function of time. It is possible to look at an object for five seconds and be overcome by its beauty. Or one may spend many minutes discovering details in an object that are not apparent at first sight.

Kenneth Clark once wrote that initially he could enjoy an esthetic sensation in front of a work of art for about as long as he could enjoy the smell of an orange—which in his case was less than two minutes. The only way he could stay longer was to look attentively at different aspects of the painting or sculpture

Michelangelo Buonarroti
The Academy Slaves.
Probably carved 1527–28, from blocks cut 1516–20.
"Bearded" Slave
(detail, below):
marble, height 8′4¾″;
"Blockhead" Slave
(opposite): marble, height 8′7½″.
Accademia di Belle Arti, Florence

Overleaf:
Michelangelo Buonarroti
David.
1501–4.
Marble, height 14′3″.
Galleria dell'Accademia, Florence

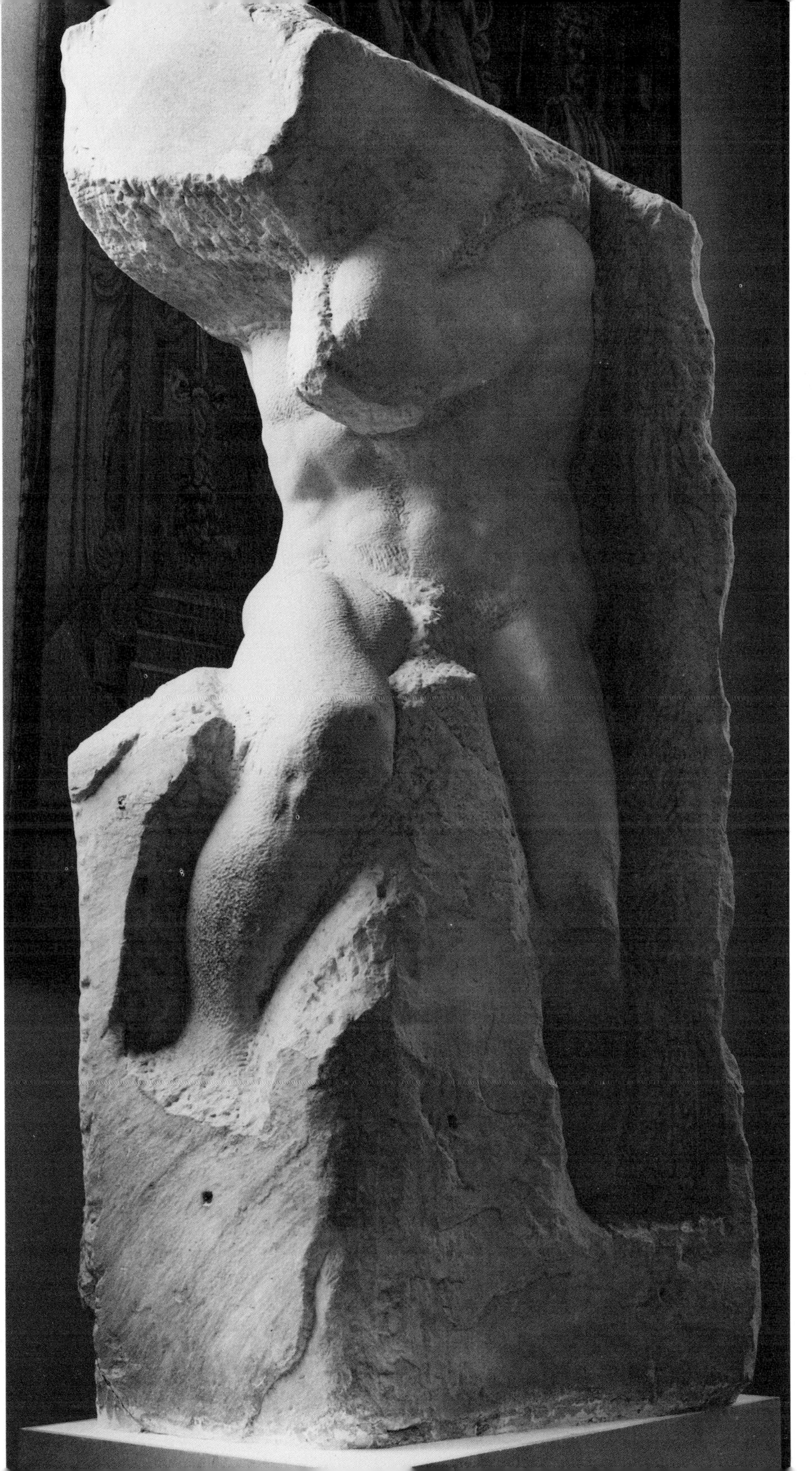

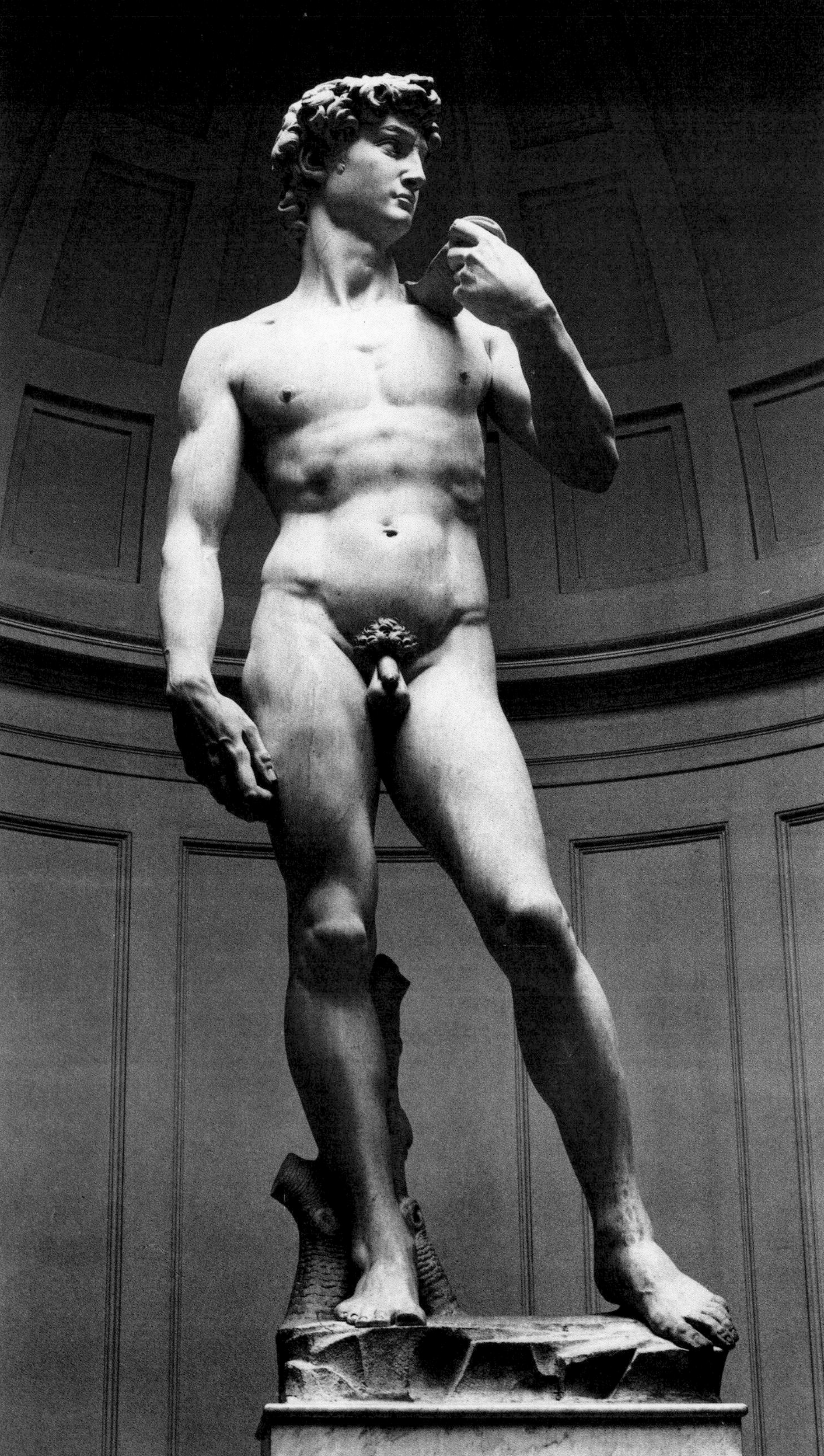

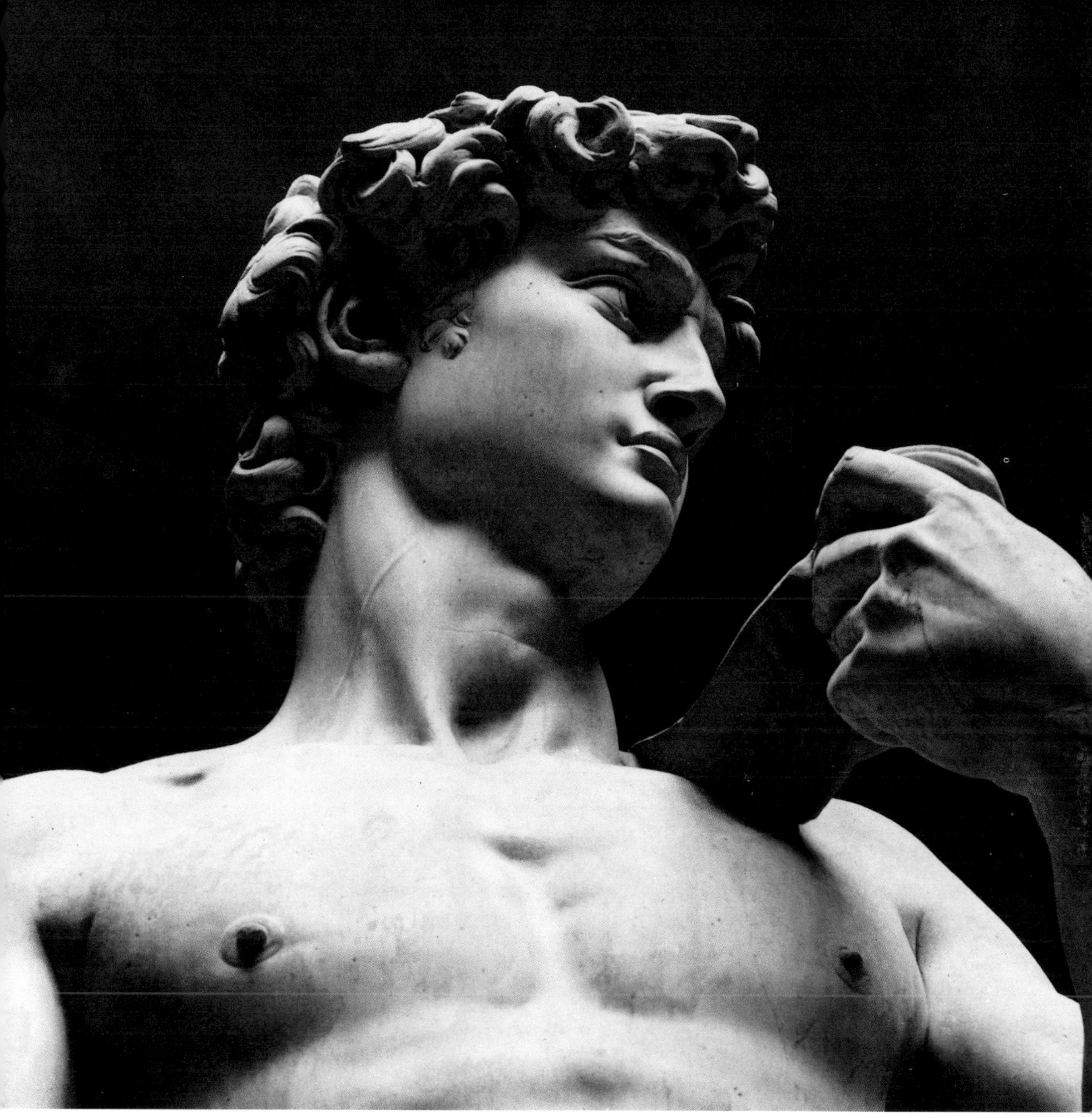

and "fortify himself with nips of information" about both the artist and the work, until finally he became "saturated" with it. To emphasize the importance of looking carefully at each section of a painting to discover its deeper qualities, he published two volumes of his favorite details from paintings in the National Gallery in London.

You probably will not have a chance to become *saturated* with an individual work of art on your first visit to a great museum. Even in two or three hours you will probably not find it possible to do more than glance at each of the works on display. But if one or two strike you as really exciting, stay a little longer and enjoy the experience of discovering beautiful forms in the details.

A scientist I know developed his own approach to absorbing the qualities of a work of art. He took a six-month leave of absence to travel around the world and broaden his cultural horizons, and spent hours in museums trying to absorb the richness of individual works of art. He told me that he would sit in front of a painting studying all its parts until he thought he knew it thoroughly; then he would close his eyes and try to reconstruct in his mind's eye what was there. Usually he found that he could not remember certain sections of the painting, so he would open his eyes and examine those parts more carefully. He would repeat the exercise until he satisfied himself that he knew the whole painting.

The main advantage of this unusual idea is that it makes one *look* carefully at what is there, and if one *looks* hard there is a good chance one will learn to *see*. It is not the memorizing itself that is important, but the deep response within oneself to what the artist created. If one looks at a detail of a painting and is moved by some quality one finds there—the masterly rendition of an object, or the exquisite combination of colors, or the fascinating interplay of forms, or the portrayal of a human experience, or the ingenious creation of a mood, or the presentation of a brilliant idea—or something one cannot put one's finger on but finds somehow extraordinarily exciting—then one is *seeing* rather than just *looking*. Any technique that can help rivet one's eyes on a work of art for more than a few seconds increases the chance of having such an experience. And it is that experience which makes art something of great value in human life.

YOU CAN ENJOY A VARIETY OF STYLES AND PERIODS. We live in a time when there are more and more categories of art that we can learn to enjoy. In the late nineteenth century, academic art was the rage, and the French Impressionists were the unpopular rebels. Then, earlier in the twentieth century the situation was reversed: academic art was scorned and the Impressionists were beloved by all. Now we enjoy both. Fifty years ago, Bernini and Canova were considered the epitome of wrong-headed sculptors; today they are revered. The pre-Raphaelites thought that Raphael and his followers had ruined painting for three hundred years; now we love both the pre-Raphaelites and the paintings they hated.

We also like classicists, neo-classicists, expressionists, surrealists, futurists, realists, abstract expressionists, minimalists, photorealists, conceptualists. We like African and Oceanic art, pre-Columbian art, Greek and Roman art, Romanesque, Gothic, and Renaissance art.

Some people go only to see early American furniture, or the decorative arts. There are some who have a passion for armor, some for majolica dishes or Limoges enamels, others for ivory carvings, still others for medieval manuscripts. Prints and drawings attract many enthusiasts, as do exhibitions of photographs and displays of magnificent jewels. That is the advantage of the great museums—not that any of us can expect to see and appreciate everything, but that we can dwell on those kinds of things that mean the most to us. And we can expand our horizon of esthetic interests by looking at all kinds of objects as we head for our own favorites.

Our ability to appreciate so many different schools of art is a blessing. It is perhaps the reward of living in the first truly global era of history. But this openness to different periods of art does not diminish our right to have personal preferences.

The classic remark "I don't know much about art, but I know what I like" is not as dumb as some people think. Knowing what you like is far more important than knowing what you are *supposed* to like. And knowing what you *dislike* is as important as knowing what you *like*. You have to make judgments when walking through a museum, and be able to say, "I don't care for such and such, but I do enjoy these." Discrimination is a necessary component of appreciation.

Each of us has somewhat different tastes. It is not true that great art is great because its values are universal and enduring. Judgments about art are *never* unanimous, and they change—sometimes radically—from age to age. No artist's place is secure in posterity. Tastes vary from individual to individual and change constantly with the passage of time. And

Raphael
Madonna of the Chair
(detail). 1514–15.
Oil on panel, diameter 28″.
Pitti Palace, Florence

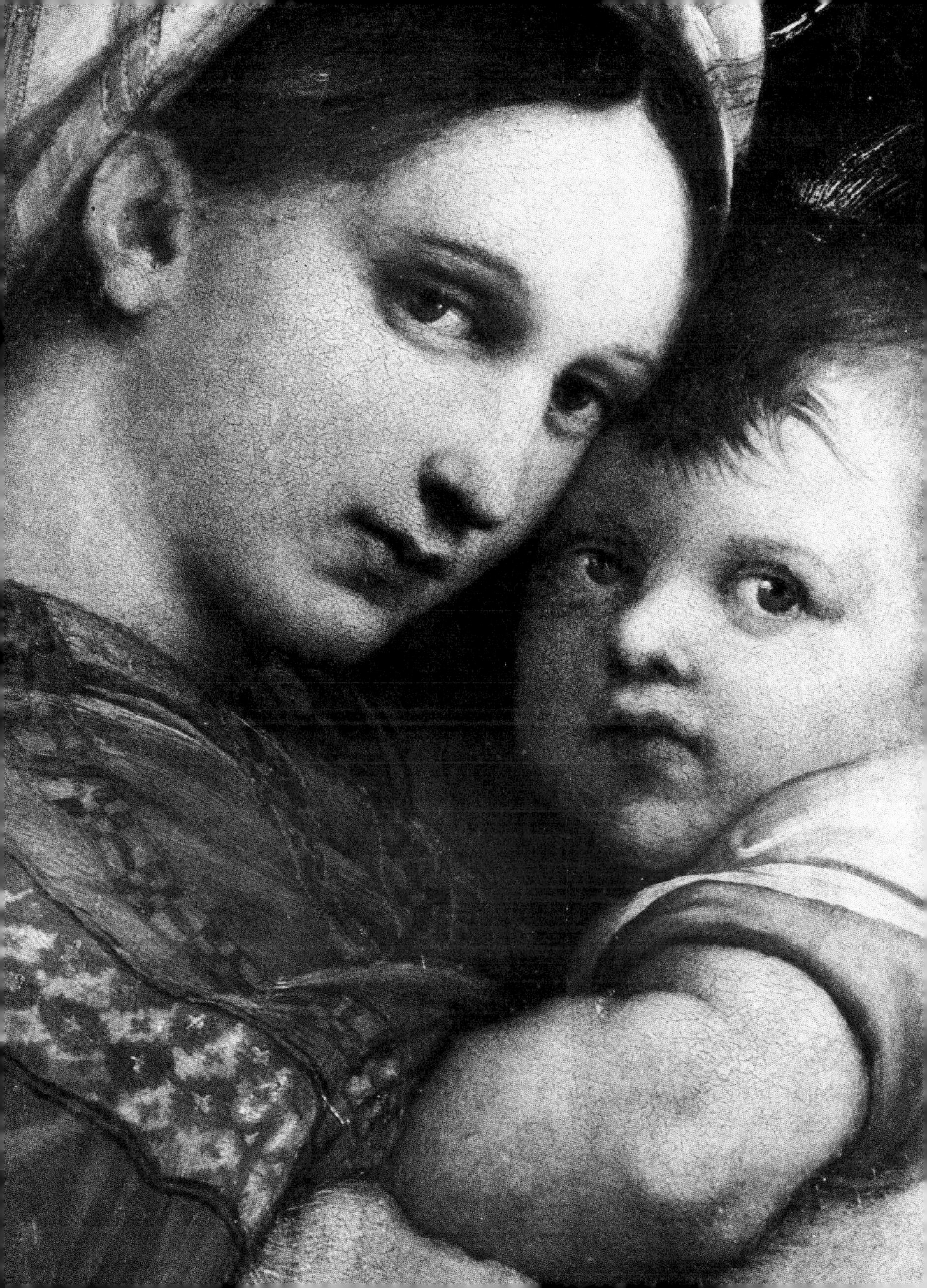

inevitably this affects our enjoyment of and response to particular works of art.

THE JOYS OF MAKING YOUR OWN DISCOVERIES. In looking at any massive collection of paintings there is a tendency to ignore works by artists whose names you do not recognize. Yet any canvas painted hundreds of years ago that has been preserved this long must in some way be worth looking at. If you try to look at the work of at least two or three unfamiliar painters with a fresh eye whenever you walk through a museum, you will learn about artists who may come to mean a great deal to you.

The pleasure of discovering masterpieces by unfamiliar artists has an interesting counterpart in the tendency to pay too much attention to the works of famous artists. This is a problem common to all the arts. Franz Liszt once played two compositions at a concert—one by Beethoven and a second by a lesser-known composer; but he reversed the announced sequence to test the audience. There was a storm of applause for what was considered Beethoven and only polite applause for the other. It is a universal weakness to admire works by famous artists just because they are famous and to ignore those by unknown artists.

Seeing many works by a well-known artist can help one appreciate his greatness. Each new painting adds to the total understanding of the work as a whole. Just the same, it is best to guard against the tendency to say to yourself, "Oh, that's a Botticelli," and move on to the next painting as if the act of recognition were an end in itself. You will get much more out of the painting if you push the name of the painter to the back of your mind and look at the work itself to see what might stimulate your esthetic juices.

One does tend to fall in love with a particular artist when one sees his great masterpieces. Yet at the same time it can be difficult to know how to deal with a work that has become such an esthetic celebrity that you can hardly see past its fame. A friend told me that she once overheard a father pointing out a Cézanne painting to his young son, saying, "Now, *that's* a great painting!" "Why?" asked the boy. "Because it was painted by a great painter," replied the father. "Why was he a great painter?" asked the persistent son. "Because," the father answered, "he painted great paintings."

Just glancing at Leonardo da Vinci's *Mona Lisa* in the Louvre brings to mind the numberless cheap reproductions and parodies one sees so often. One way to overcome the glorification of a particular work of art is to concentrate on some of the details and see what you can discover with a fresh eye. The Mona Lisa's features are so delicately painted—the eyes, the nose, the mouth. The hands are so sensitively rendered in their graceful position in front of the figure. The landscape in the background is so darkly mysterious. Above all, the painting quality is so luminous; there is an eerie sense of airiness within, as if one could walk into three-dimensional space. By focusing on such aspects of a work of art, one can see past its fame and appreciate its inner qualities.

Overleaf:
Leonardo da Vinci
Mona Lisa. c. 1503–5.
Oil on panel, 30¼ x 21″.
The Louvre, Paris

LET YOUR EYE, NOT THE WALL LABEL, GUIDE YOU. Should you look at the identifying label first, or look at the object first? If you know the artist and the period in advance, it gives you

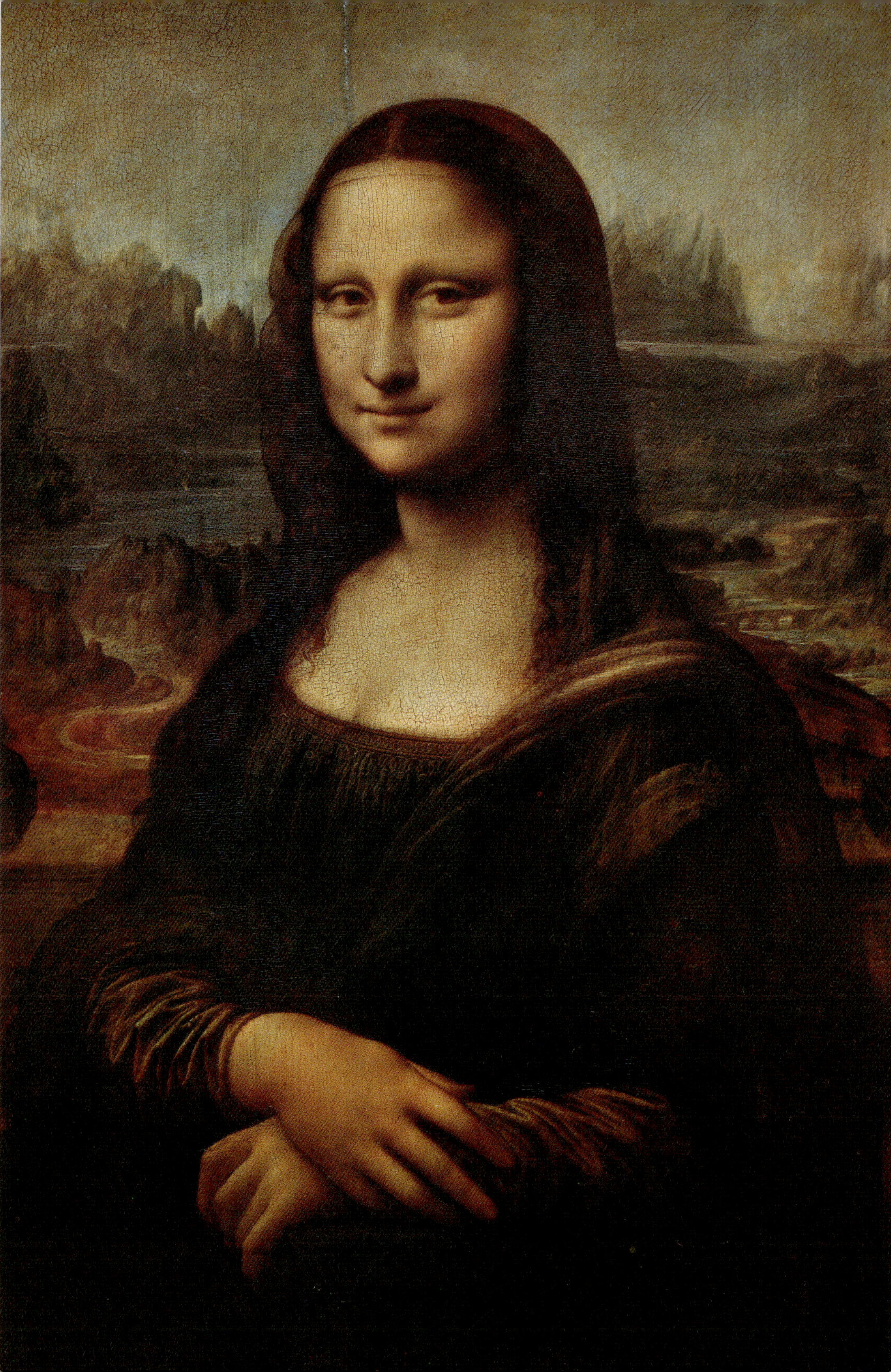

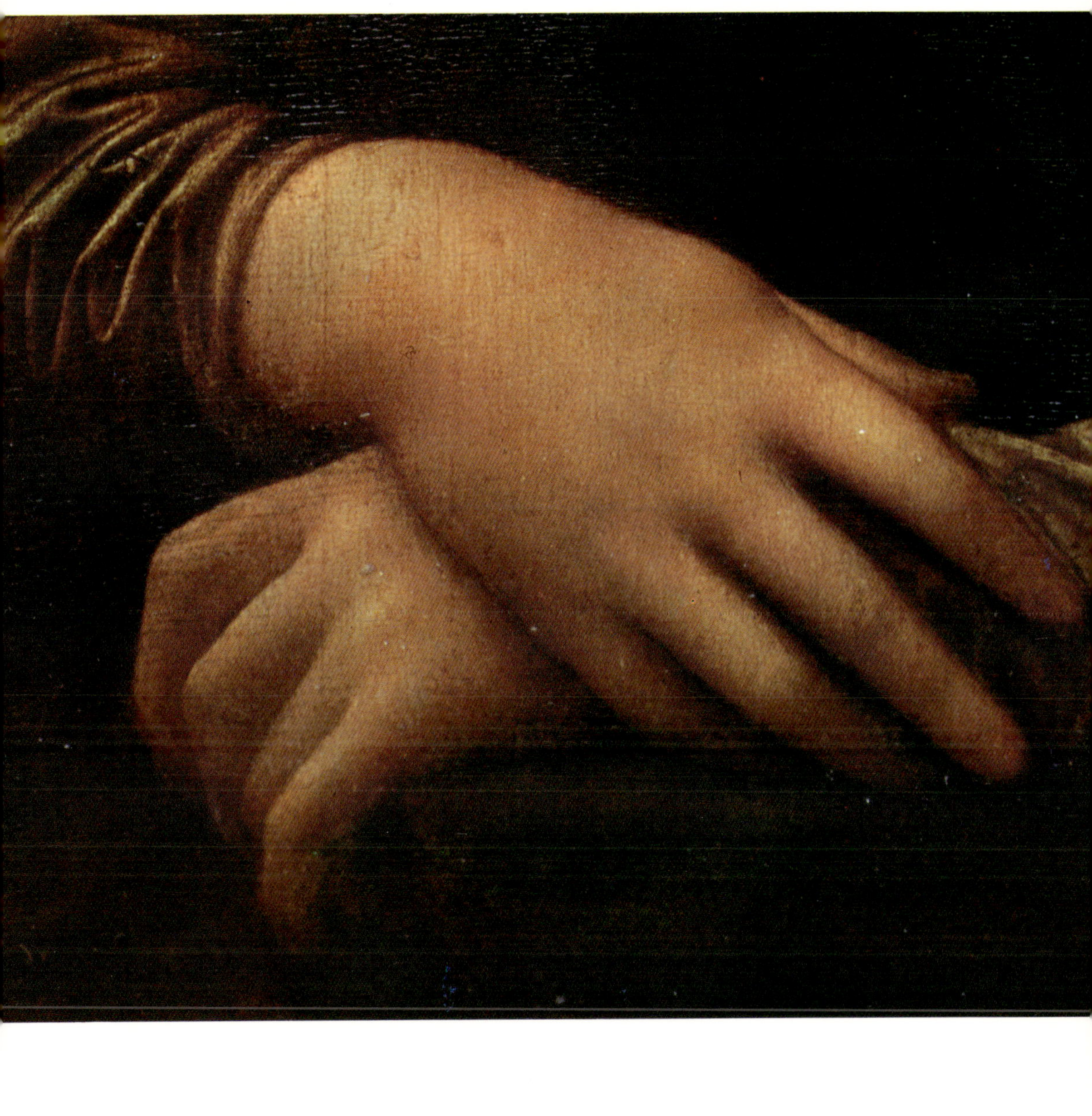

a certain mind-set with which to look at the work. But sometimes you find yourself paying more attention to the information about the object than the object itself. This is at best a way to learn a little about art history, but not about art. Museum professionals disagree about whether labels are an aid or a distraction to viewers. Many European museums simply label works with a number that refers to a catalogue entry, while some American museums place a long description next to the painting.

Each person must find the best way to cope with the question of whether and when to read labels. One approach is to walk around the galleries rather quickly but with a high degree of concentration, sometimes looking at labels first but trying hard to look at each work of art to see if there is anything there that especially attracts your eye. The trick is to discipline yourself not to pay much attention to works that do *not* seem to speak to you at this particular moment, recognizing that your mood is always different from one museum visit to another. The work of an artist who means a great deal to you on some occasions might find you indifferent on others. Your object is to enjoy *this* visit, so look for those works that appeal most to you *now,* and read their labels carefully.

You will probably end up with a mixture of works by well-known artists and a few by artists you knew little or nothing about before. But if you have followed your instincts, these will be works that especially move you. Perhaps you will look carefully at one out of every ten or twenty works, with only a handful in the entire museum making a truly profound impression.

The most successful museum visits are those on which you come across one overwhelming work. It might be a different one on different visits to the same museum, depending on your mood, but when that explosion takes place the experience is almost unbearable. A powerful experience in front of one great work of art can make a museum visit totally fulfilling. If you are lucky enough to have such a supreme moment, the thrill of seeing a masterpiece will be felt throughout your entire being.

FRAMING DETAILS IN YOUR MIND'S EYE. These days one can see visitors with camera flashes popping off every few seconds in many museums. Even where there are official prohibitions against the use of artificial lights in order to protect the works of art, the amateur photographer with his automatic camera can usually snap away at will. Obviously the visitors are trying to take back with them some record of a painting or sculpture they enjoyed, but what do those prints or slides look like when they come back from the local drugstore? Paintings above eye level will be badly distorted by parallax (the converging of vertical lines). Paintings at eye level may be blotted out by the reflection of the flash. Objects photographed in glass cases will tend to be hidden by reflections. At best, the ordinary snapshot will be little more than a memento.

There is, however, another value in aiming one's viewfinder at a work of art that strikes you as being particularly beautiful. Seeing the work framed in the camera lens offers a different experience from seeing it with the naked eye. This is particularly true when

Overleaf:
Piero della Francesca
Nativity. c. 1470.
Panel, 49 x 48½″.
National Gallery, London

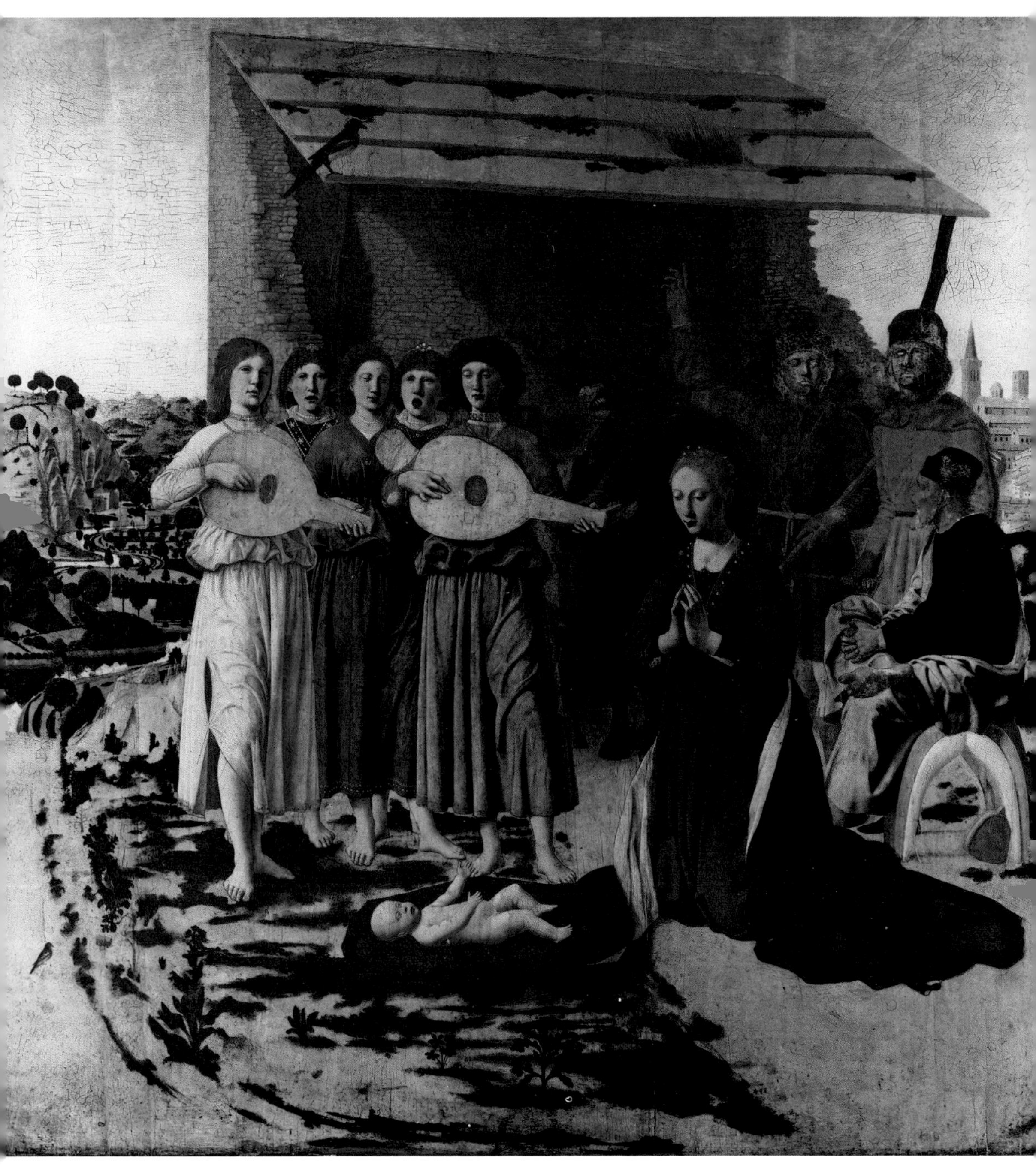

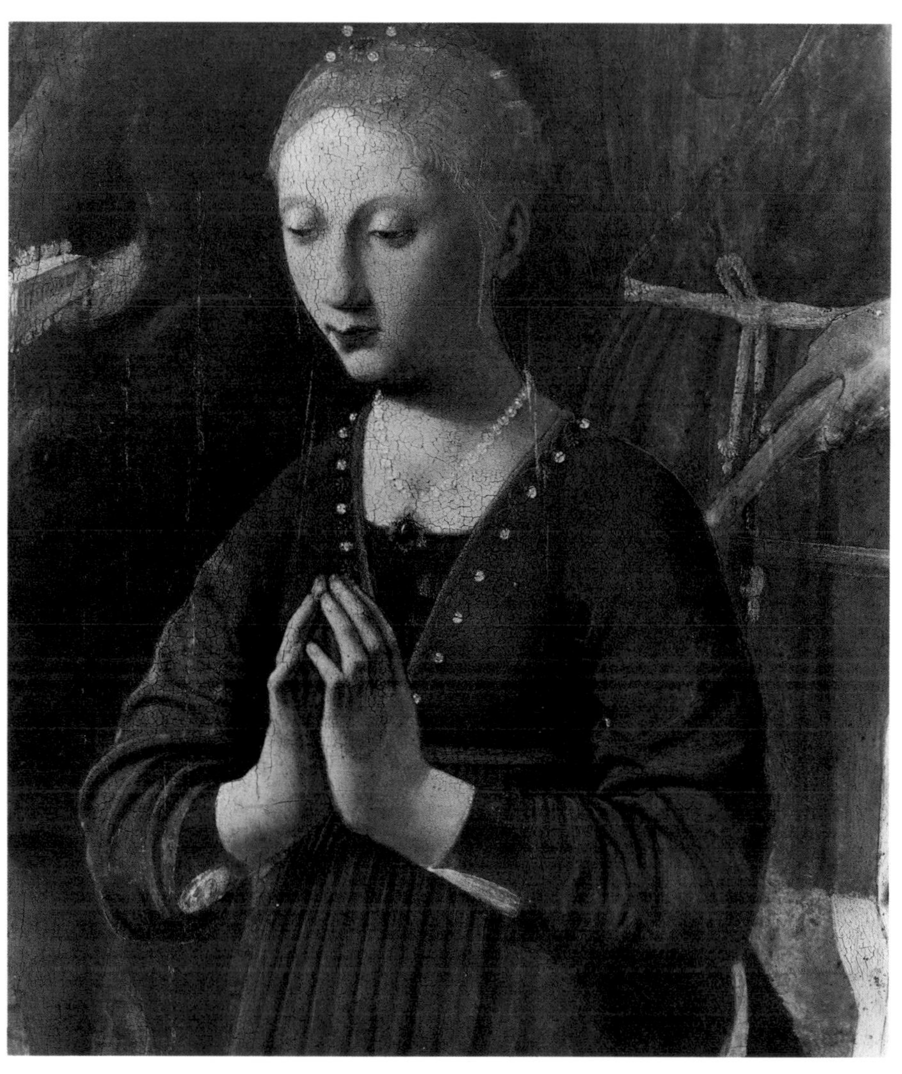

aiming the camera at details of a painting, or searching out what you particularly enjoyed when you were looking at the work of art. And this can be especially meaningful as you reflect back on your visit.

Sometimes even better than a camera is a compact pair of opera glasses that you can keep in your pocket or pocketbook. The virtue of opera glasses is that you can see details close up. As you look at section after section of a painting, you will find many details you would have missed without the kind of concentration that opera glasses make possible.

Still another technique is the practice of sketching a painting or sculpture. This can be even more rewarding than photographing or looking through opera glasses, because when one draws an object one studies every detail. Artists and art students always used to draw from works of art as a way of training their eye, and a few still do. Every now and then one sees a painter sitting behind an easel in a museum, or a passer-by making some quick notes in a sketchbook. Even if one is not very accomplished, it is still worthwhile to make the effort. The pencil acts like a magnifying glass, focusing one's eye on marvelous things that might otherwise be overlooked.

BRINGING THE MUSEUM INTO YOUR HOME. A stop at the museum bookshop at the end of your visit can provide items that will help you remember some of the beautiful things you have seen and become worthwhile references for future trips.

Also, you may discover while browsing at the end of a visit that there is some extraordinary work in the collection you somehow missed seeing. Because of such experiences, some people stop in the museum shop at the beginning of a visit in order to get an idea of what to look for. Of course, sometimes choice paintings or sculptures are located in rooms one misses as one wanders through a museum, or they may not even be on display. But you cannot let such disappointments affect the pleasure of your visit. What you do not see is never as important as what you do.

Slides and reproductions of paintings and sculpture are popular with many museum-goers, and most museum shops have extensive collections of both. Reproductions enable one to live with a work of art in one's own home. It is not the same as the original, but close enough to provide a great deal of esthetic pleasure. If you want a reproduction of a painting or sculpture or even a drawing for which there is no postcard, order a photograph from the museum, which usually has prints available.

If you are a book collector, catalogues of the museum collection are wonderful to take away with you. By reading catalogues after you have visited the museum, you can learn more about the works that impressed you most. The great works will be fully documented (and sometimes reproduced) in the catalogue, and there will be something too about the lesser-known works that you "discovered" on your own.

As you leave the museum, you will find that no matter how much or little time you spent, you saw some things in your visit that were rewarding. Your spirit will be uplifted, your mind enriched with new images, your sensitivity to the visual world enhanced. In this way, visits to museums become a significant part of your life.

TO BE OR NOT TO BE ALONE

Do people go to museums more often with friends than alone? Museum-going seems to be largely a communal or at least a sharing experience. If you walk around the galleries of almost any museum, you see couples or families or groups wandering around together. The solitary individuals are more the exception than the rule.

There is no question that the opportunity to tell a friend what you have discovered in a painting or sculpture enhances the experience. Sometimes when you are alone and see something exquisitely beautiful, there is a feeling of incompleteness in not being able to communicate the sensation to another. There is an urge to say, "Look at the marvelous line, look at the expression on the face, look at the incredible shapes the colors create on the canvas." If someone else can indeed look and see what you have seen, the greatness of the work seems more firmly embedded in your memory. It is reinforced by knowing that another person has seen it too.

One of the most pleasurable experiences in museum-going is when husband and wife—or two close friends—are together. Perhaps this is because being exposed to a work of art can touch the deepest chords of one's being. Sharing the experience with someone close to you strengthens the bond between kindred spirits. This is true of other esthetic experi-

The Ashmolean Museum, Oxford

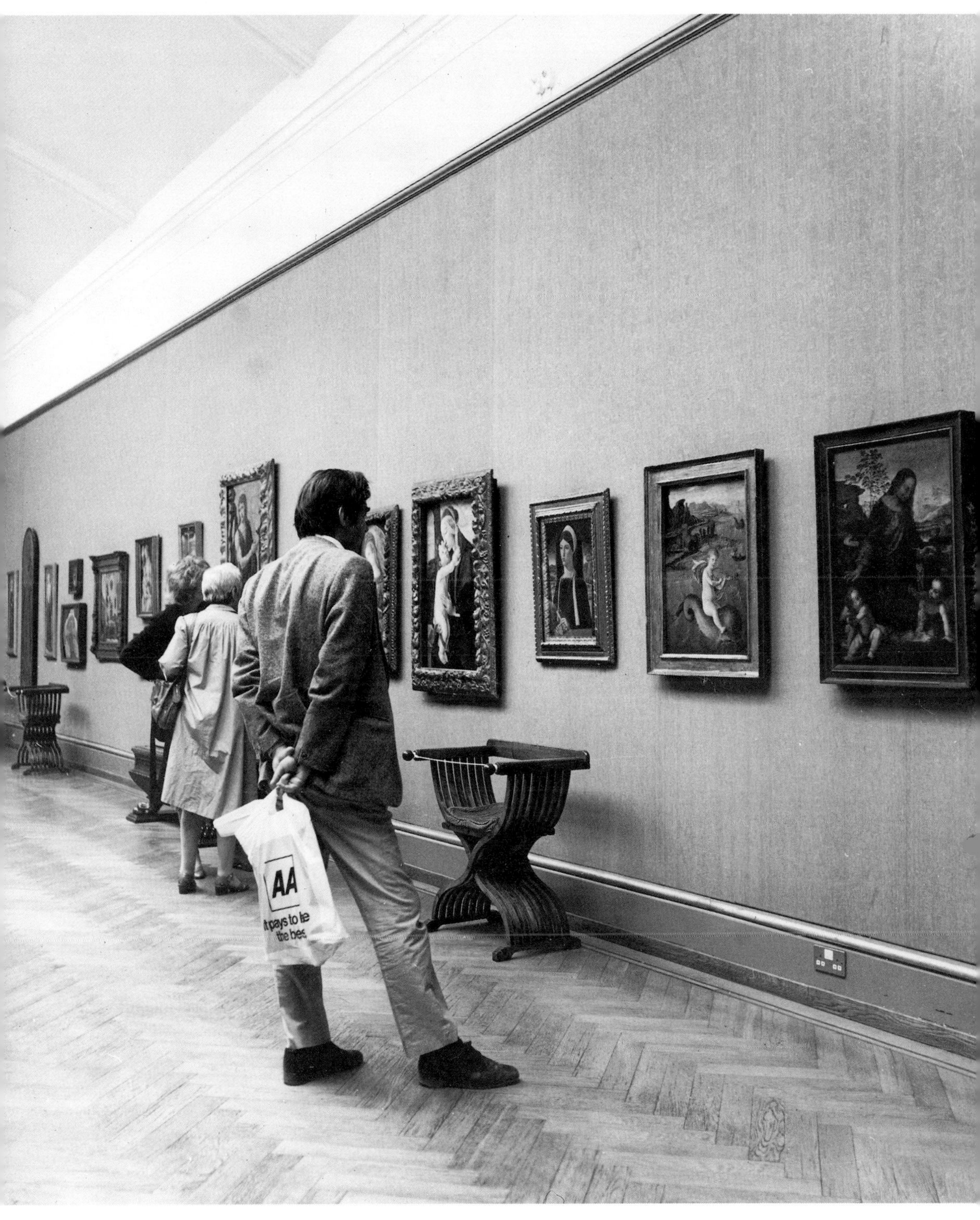
AA
It pays to be
the bes

ences that have a communal aspect to them—theater, music, dance, film. Even if you read a book that has a powerful effect, you probably are eager to persuade close friends to read it as well. Today, watching television with others in the family is often more satisfying than watching alone.

The added virtue of being in a museum with a close companion is the feedback each can give the other. Four eyes can see more than two. This can be a godsend when you are in a place like the Sistine Chapel in the Vatican. If two people exchange discoveries, they can find features in the great Michelangelo frescoes and the paintings that line the walls that either one of them might have missed. They will be partners in exploration, and between them see far more than either could alone.

Often one sees couples walking around with one partner reading aloud from a guidebook and the other looking at the works of art. When the reader looks up, the other can quickly point out what seems most exciting. This helps to resolve the dilemma of how to divide one's attention between reading and seeing.

Each partner may also bring something different to the museum experience. One friend of mine who has an interest in history can stand in a spot in the Roman Forum that has nothing but a couple of old stones on the ground and conjure up in his mind's eye what was going on in that precise location a couple of thousand years ago. His trusty guidebook always in hand, he helps his wife, who has a less-developed historical sense, experience what she would never bother to read about if she were alone.

Of course, the most rewarding experience for any couple is when they discover something together and both react with the same enthusiasm. Recently my wife and I spent a couple of days in Vancouver, British Columbia, whose main art museum was temporarily closed. Just our luck, we thought, and assumed that we would miss out on the key art experience of that city. Our luck, however, was better than we thought. The taxi driver who picked us up at the airport turned out to be a young painter who had emigrated from Czechoslovakia and recently become a Canadian citizen. While asking him what made him decide to settle in Vancouver, he mentioned the Museum of Anthropology at the University of British Columbia. He told us it was an esthetic experience not to be missed. When we made the trip the next day, we discovered why. It is an architectural gem, ideally conceived to show a superb collection of carvings by Northwest Indians. The totem poles, both inside and outside the museum, are spectacularly displayed, and walking around the museum together was the high point of our trip. We spent less than an hour at the museum, but both of us found our heads spinning with the fantastic images we had seen.

Actually, we had been misinformed as to the opening time of the museum and arrived while it was still closed. We had been told at the hotel information desk that the museum opened at 10:00 A.M., and giving ourselves plenty of time, we arrived at a comfortable 11:30. To our dismay, we found a locked door with a sign announcing the opening hour as noon. Fortunately, a friendly guard urged us to walk around the museum where, he said, there were many lovely things to see. Sauntering along a winding path and through a thick grove of trees, we came upon an open field at the rear of the museum. There, a number of wonderful totem poles and some Indian buildings with fine carvings gave us a sense of personal discovery. The back of the museum was all glass, through which we could see some of the masterpieces inside. The half hour we spent outside the museum was as rewarding as the time spent inside.

PLANNING YOUR VISIT TOGETHER. Often one partner will take the lead in planning a museum experience, doing enough homework to learn what to look for and to plan how much time to allocate to a visit. Once in the museum, a couple may or may not move around at the same pace. If they are experienced museum-goers, they may want to combine the freedom of following their own instincts with the companionship of being together. They can accomplish both by agreeing to wander from gallery to gallery on their own and periodically catch up with each other to compare notes.

The advantage of this approach is that you avoid having to walk around a museum to somebody else's drumbeat. It can kill the enjoyment of a museum visit if one person calls the tune and the other is in a different mood.

However, it is another story if you are fortunate enough to be with an inspired teacher who slows down your pace as he or she opens your eyes to things you could never see on your own. A knowledgeable museum lecturer points out aspects of a work of art that might ordinarily be overlooked, or explains something about its background that will help place it in context. The same holds true about advice from friends who are familiar with a museum you are about to visit. If they point out which rooms contain their favorite works, it gives you something specific to look for, and their enthusiasm heightens your sense of anticipation.

The value of expert guidance is, of course, the theory behind organized tours or lectures in museums. Many museums have extensive docent programs, providing trained guides to take people through the galleries. This works well when the guides have a real feeling for the works they are describing, but can be very frustrating if they do not. Particularly distressing are museums that force one to take the guided tour. Usually the guides have told their stories so often that they mechanically make the points they are supposed to make and focus on getting the group out on time so the next one can begin on schedule.

I usually try to separate myself from the crowd on tours of this sort in order to concentrate on works that I find most interesting. Tour guides can become very impatient with such behavior. I remember a group going through the Raphael Loggias in the Vatican when a member of the group stayed behind to look closely at one of the paintings, and was told curtly: "No loitering, please!" Looking at the art was a distraction from the main business of the tour, which was to listen to the guide's deadening recital.

Audioguides may vary in quality as much as live guides, although the former are likely to be more authoritative. There are times when they are invaluable, especially when one wants information about a particular artist or group of works. The disadvantage of audioguides, however, is that they take you through a museum at the speaker's pace, and, because you are being told what to look for in each work of art, you may not have the same sense of personal discovery that you can get when you are on your own.

Whether or not to use an audioguide is, therefore, a question of mood and place.

Arms and Armor Room in the Metropolitan Museum of Art, New York

ART AND MUSIC. Speaking of mood, there is a role that the accompaniment of music can play in special museum exhibitions, just as there is in films on art. Musical performances are sometimes arranged at exhibition openings in order to provide such a background. Some museum visitors enjoy hearing their favorite Bach, Beethoven, or Brahms on a pocket tape recorder with earphones as they walk around the galleries.

HELPING CHILDREN ENJOY THEIR VISITS. Any discussion of museum visiting in groups must include some reference to the experience of going with children. Young people need help from an adult who can tell them something about a painting or sculpture that will stimulate their interest. Telling stories about works of art helps them pay attention to what they are seeing. They need to be entertained as well as artistically stimulated.

When taking children to museums it is always best to approach works of art in their terms rather than with an adult point of view. The powerful impact of a Cézanne still life may not strike their unpracticed eyes, but their interest may be piqued by talking about the fruit on the table, reminding them that sometimes there is fruit like that on the table at home, asking if the apples look good enough to eat or whether it makes them hungry to look at the painting. When looking at a Chinese watercolor, children may enjoy counting the petals on a flower. Remember that

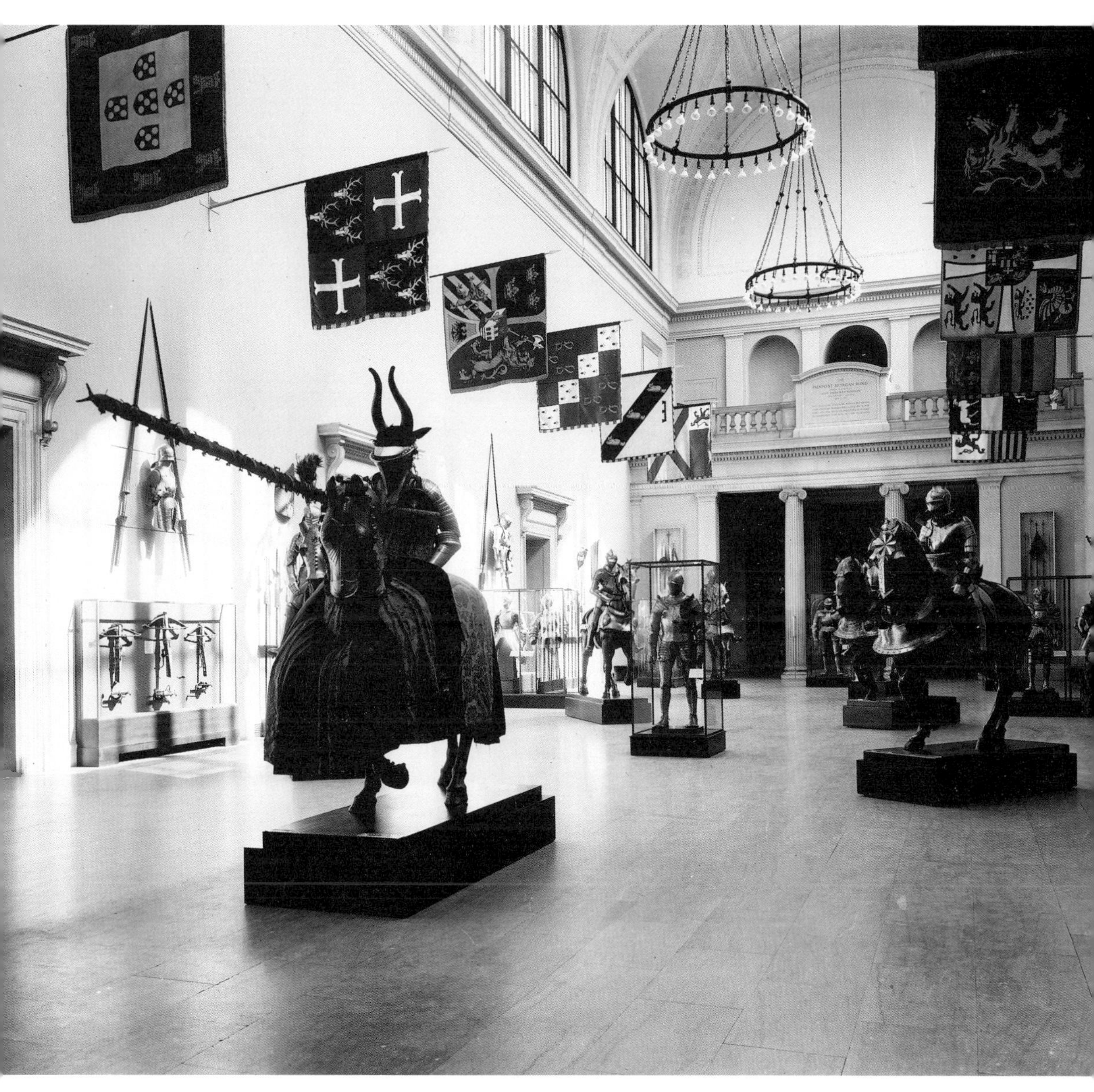

children enjoy looking at picture books, especially if parents can help weave stories around the pictures. It is this same approach that is most likely to make museum-going an enjoyable experience for children.

There are certain sections of a museum that are likely to be special favorites of children, and they should be included on a visit whenever possible. Exhibitions of armor are likely to be exciting since young people can personally identify with the knights of old and imagine themselves actually wearing those exotic objects. Period rooms may be enjoyable for similar reasons—especially extravagant settings that can give a child a sense of what it was like to live in a different place at a different time. And if they have a chance to visit an outdoor sculpture garden, where it is permitted, they may have a wonderful time romping over the fields and climbing on the large works.

ALONE. As rewarding as it is to visit museums with family, friends, or teachers, the experience of going there by oneself may leave a deeper impression. When you are on your own you are likely to be in closer communion with individual works of art and discover what it is that moves you most profoundly.

The poet Robert Browning described how he first fell in love with great works of art on his visits to the Dulwich Gallery: ". . . that Gallery I so love and am so grateful to—having been used to going there when a child, far under the age allowed by the regulations— those two Guidos, the wonderful Rembrandt of Jacob's vision, such a Watteau, the triumphant three Murillo pictures, a Giorgione music-lesson group, all the Poussins with the 'Armida' and Jupiter's nursing—and—no end to 'ands'—I have sate before one, some of those pictures I had predetermined to see, a good hour and then gone away. . . ."

If one learns early to visit museums by oneself, and repeats the experience through the years, these private experiences can play an important role in the maturing process. When I was a boy, I thought primitive Italian painting was atrocious. I would always skip the first few rooms of any museum that exhibited early European art and considered those paintings of historical rather than esthetic interest. Now I find those paintings exquisitely beautiful, and I can see why *The Avignon Pietà* is considered by some to be the most beautiful painting in the Louvre. I feel the same way about medieval sculpture and find the raw simplicity of those marvelous works immensely mov-

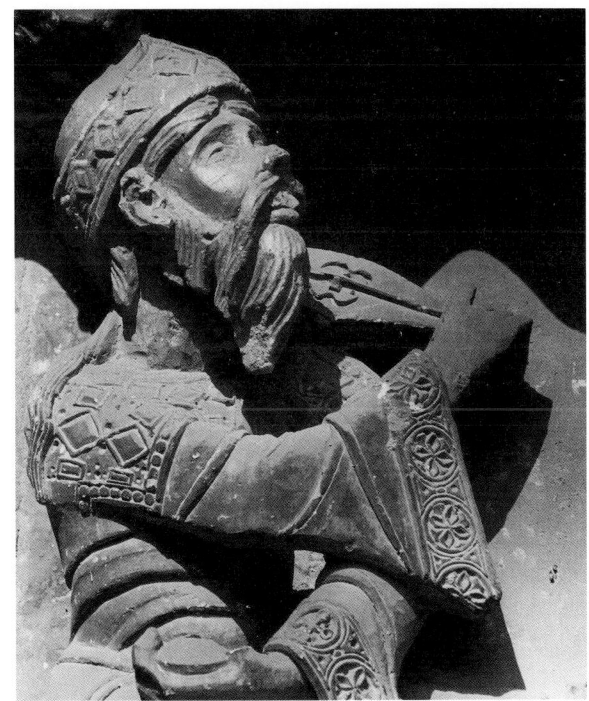

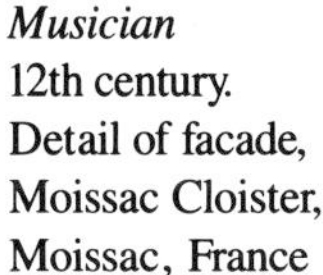

Musician
12th century.
Detail of facade,
Moissac Cloister,
Moissac, France

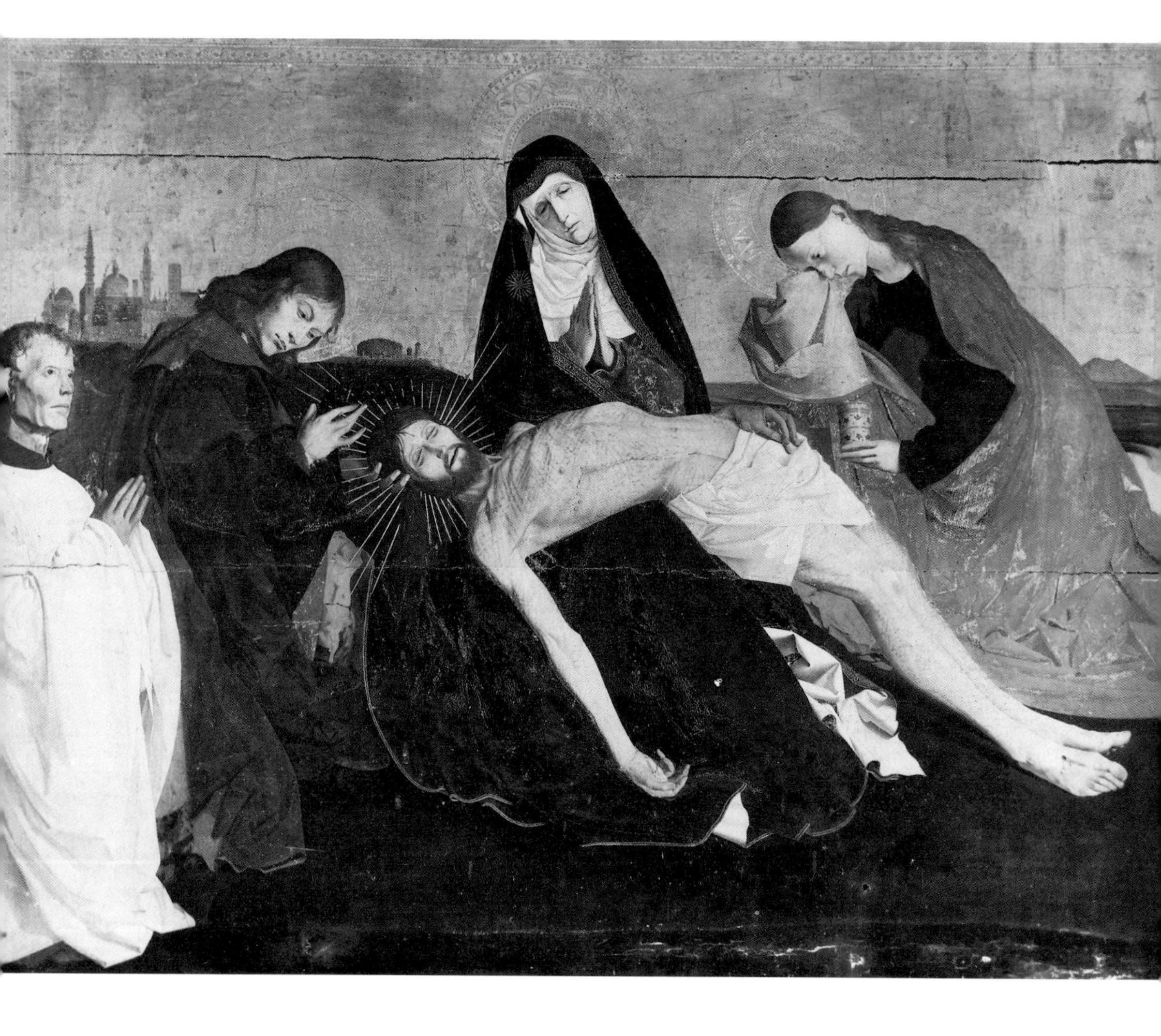

Southern French Master
The Avignon Pietà. c. 1470.
Oil on panel, 64 x 86″.
The Louvre, Paris

Right: Detail

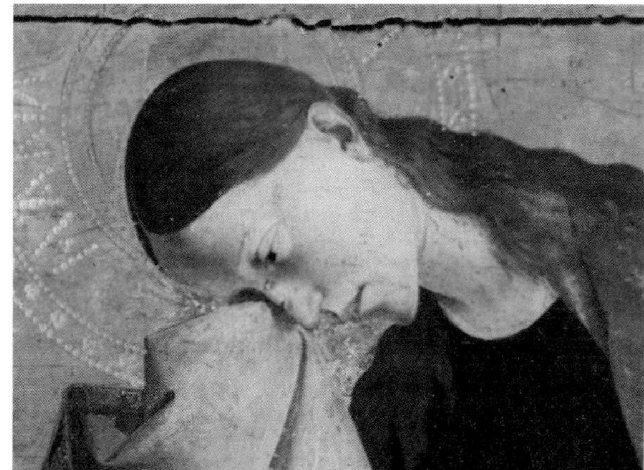

ing. But I have also learned to love the gentleness of Canova, the unabashed sentimentality of the Victorian artists, the sense of eternity in Egyptian sculpture, the monumentality of Greek figures—none of which meant much to me in my early years as a museum-goer.

There is no substitute for the vibrations that make each of us as individuals respond to a work of art. Alone with a work of art that touches our deepest feelings, our very being resonates with what we see. I cannot explain why certain works by Rembrandt or Rubens strike me as being masterpieces; or why Rouault's profoundly religious paintings almost never fail to move me; or why the silent, lonely scenes by Edward Hopper strike such a deep chord in my soul; or why Emil Nolde's richly colorful paintings seem so stunning; or why I find the late watercolors of Cézanne the epitome of pure beauty. Nor can I describe my emotions when I stand before Cellini's perfectly modeled renditions of the human figure; or Bernini's swirling forms—particularly in his terracotta bozzetti; or Marino Marini's sometimes exu-

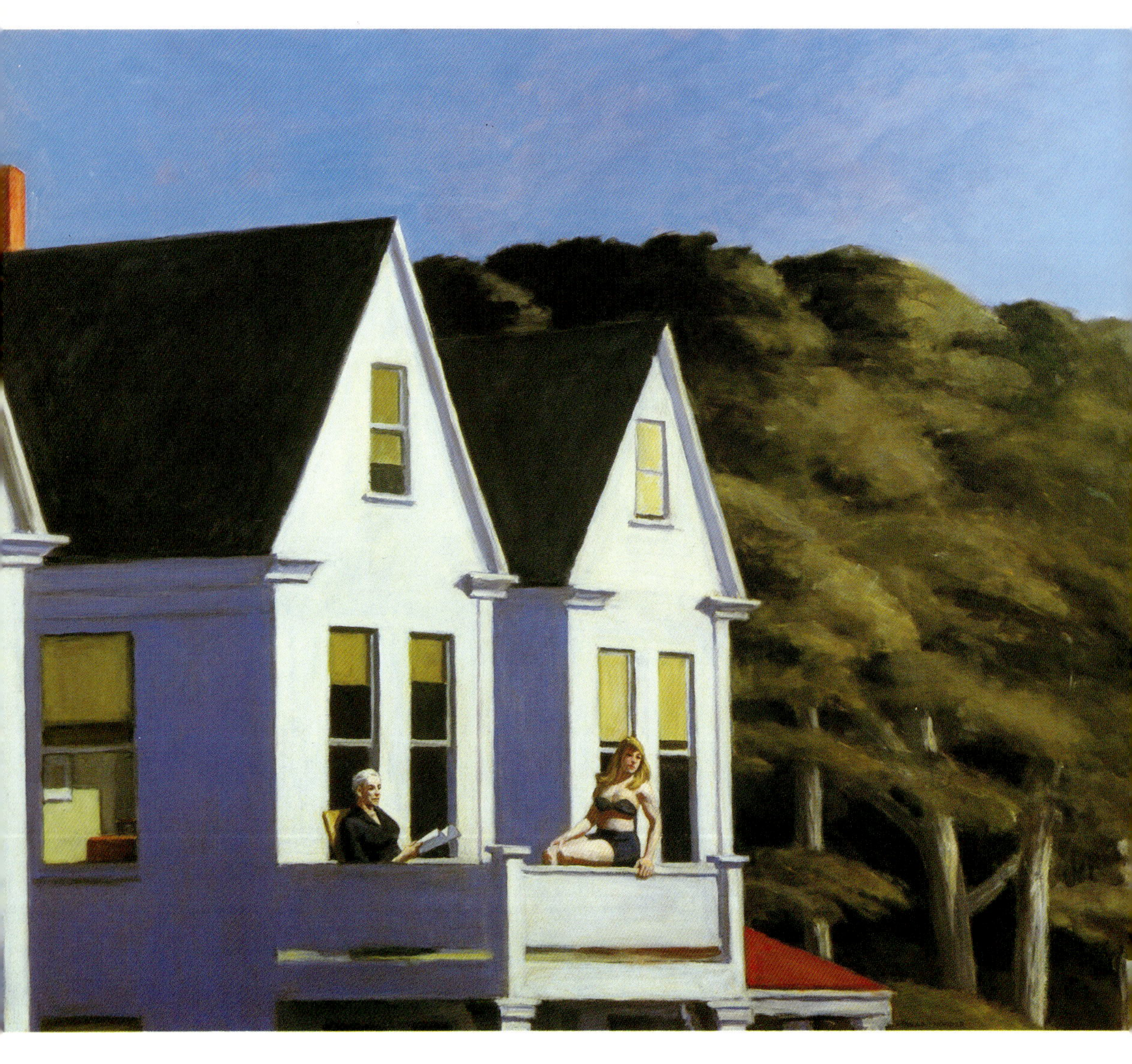

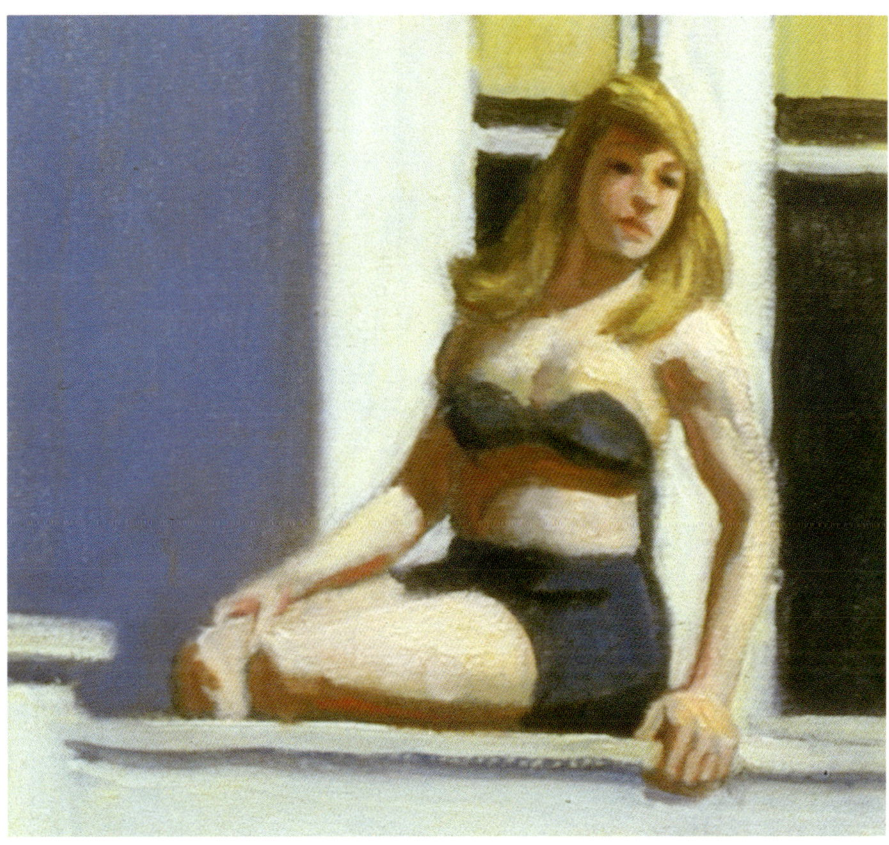

Edward Hopper
Second Story Sunlight. 1960.
Oil on canvas, 40 x 50″.
The Whitney Museum of American Art, New York. Gift of the Friends of the Whitney Museum of American Art (and purchase)

Above: Detail

berant, sometimes tragic expressions of the life force; or Henry Moore's sinuous, curving, straining, flesh-and-bone-like creations. These and so many others speak to my inner being. I have experienced their qualities so deeply that they are part of me. They are what I am.

A POWERFUL EXPERIENCE. I have had many solitary experiences that would not have been possible had I not been alone. One of the most moving occurred during a visit to the exhibition of Joseph Beuys's work at the Guggenheim Museum in 1979. It was just after a terrible tragedy had struck my family, and perhaps I was looking for solace. I had no idea what I would find, certainly not that it would be an overpowering visual and conceptual expression of the grief that was tearing me apart. I have no idea if I was reading Beuys's works correctly, but somehow I felt as if he had depicted the death of our entire civilization. Artifacts of our lives—chairs, blankets, bones, blocks of fat—all struck me as fossils carefully arranged to express metaphorically for the twentieth century what the volcanic ash had done to the ancient cities of Pompeii and Herculaneum.

Later I read the catalogue and found it of great interest, but to this day I do not know whether my response to Beuys's work was on the mark or not. I do know that it was a profound personal experience that would not have occurred if I had not been by myself and been able to react in a very personal way to what I was seeing.

DIFFERENT KINDS OF TIME. When one is by oneself one can dare to go through a museum quickly, just to get an idea of what is there. One can also dare to forget about time altogether while absorbing the marvelous qualities of a single work of art in a museum. When I have my camera with me and am taking a series of photographs of a sculpture for a book, I can spend literally hours—sometimes days—with a single work of art. This is what it was like when I was working on a book on the Bapistery doors in Florence. I knew every inch of the sculpture on those three doors by the time I was finished.

Sometimes I felt that only the sculptors and I had studied the details so thoroughly. I used to watch passers-by stop for a minute or two to look at the doors and wondered at the difference between their experience and mine.

When I am in a museum without my camera it takes more discipline to spend a lot of time with a particular work of art. Usually I need an idea to keep my eyes riveted for a long time on a painting or sculpture. For instance, I decided on one trip to the National Gallery in London to try to figure out what was so great about the Velázquez *Rokeby Venus*. I had seen the painting again and again in my walks through the gallery and had looked at reproductions in books. My reaction had been one of mild appreciation, nothing very intense. Then I came across a long poem devoted to this painting, beautifully describing its sensuous qualities. The next time I went to the museum I did nothing but stand in front of the painting, studying every detail and discovering qualities my quick once-over glances had completely missed. First of all, the idea of portraying Venus with her back toward the viewer is remarkable. The more obvious and common way to represent female beauty is to show a frontal view—with breasts, belly, face. In this painting there is simply a back. But what a beautiful back it is! Every ripple of flesh is filled with sensuousness—from the heel to the calf of the leg, the folds of skin behind the knee, the whisper of a highlight in the thigh under the buttock, the dimples in the lower back, the curve of the spine, the shoulder blades, the languorous arm propping up the head. And the rear profile of the face with just the cheek showing is so young and sensitive. The whole figure is placed luxuriously on a black silk coverlet, with a

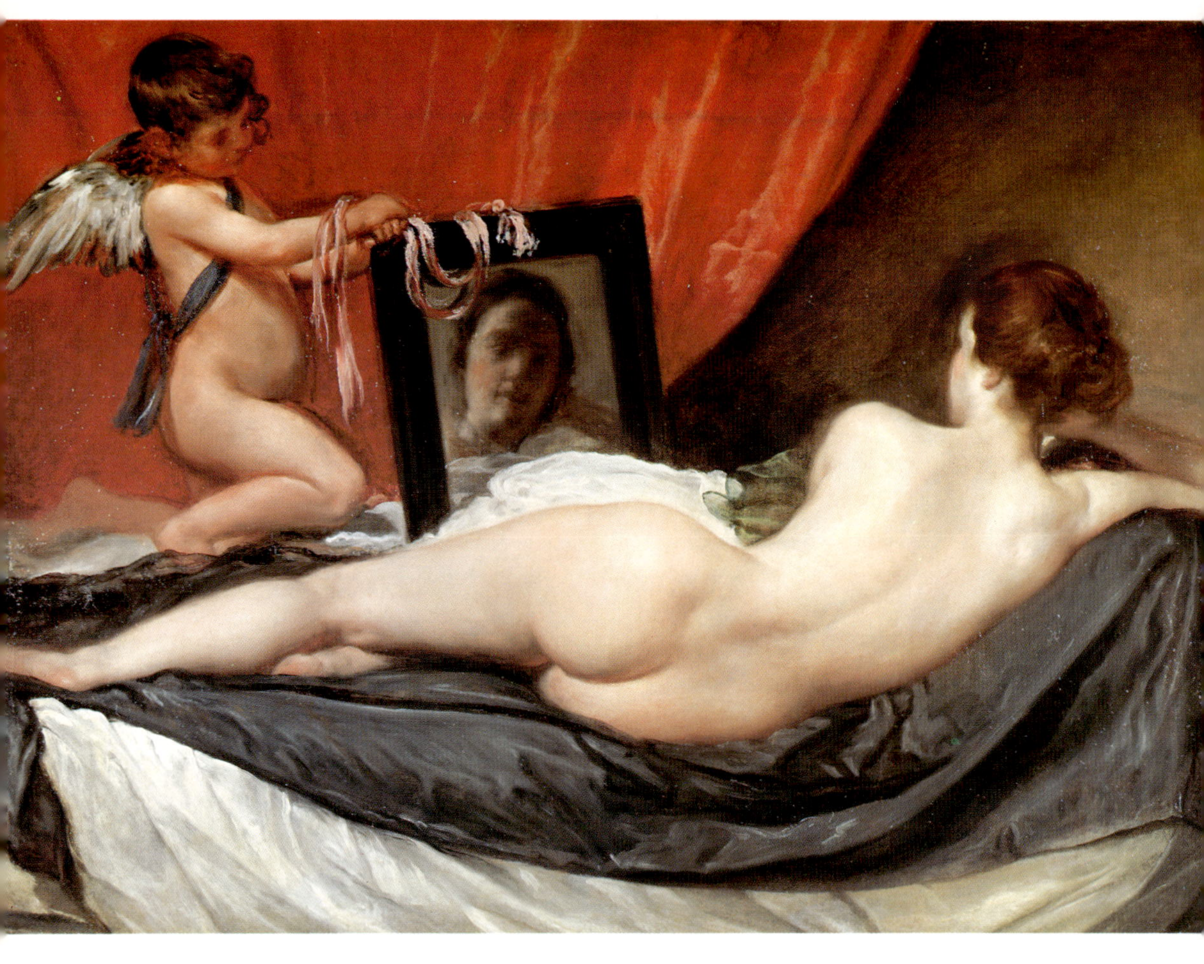

Diego Velázquez
The Toilet of Venus (The Rokeby Venus). c. 1649–50.
Oil on canvas, 48¼ x 69¾″.
National Gallery, London

Opposite: Detail

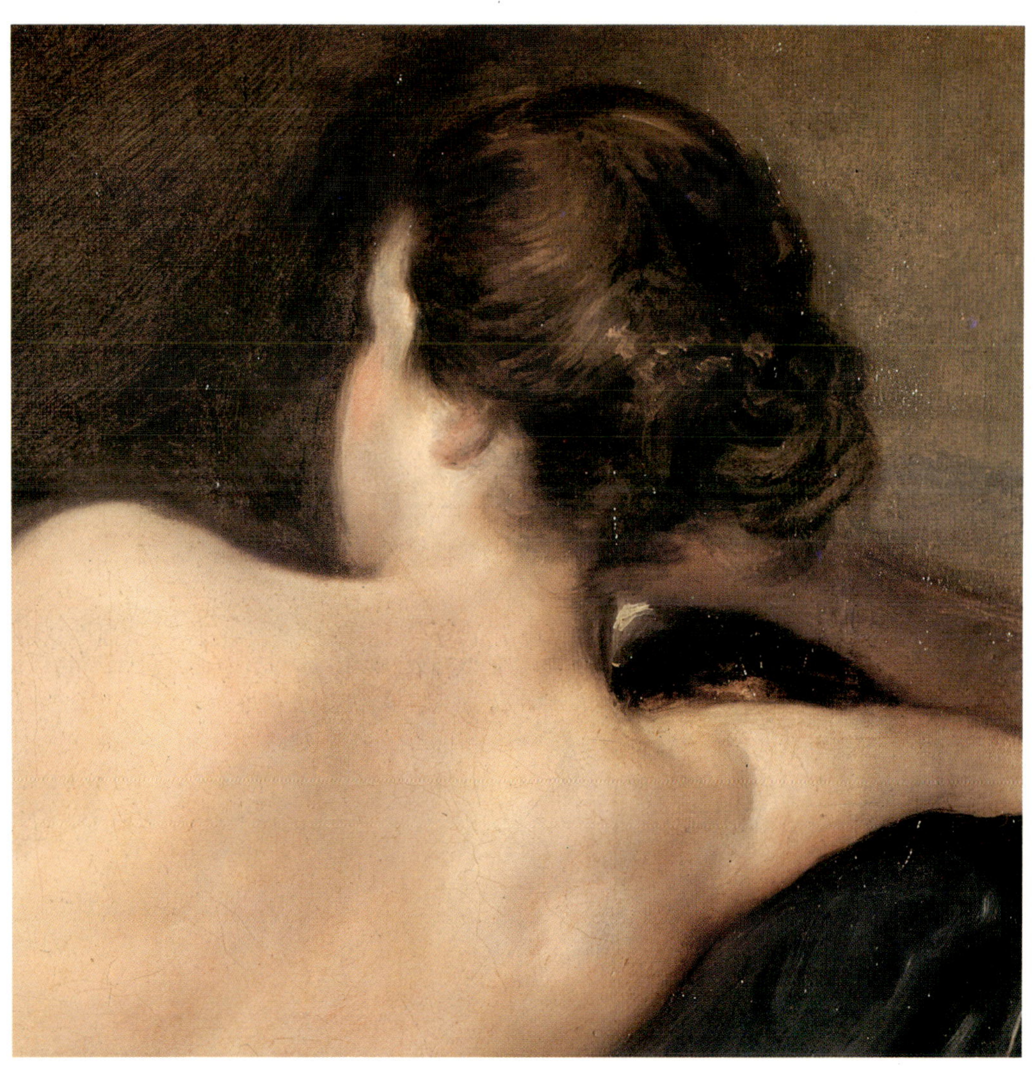

white sheet below and a rich red curtain behind. And then the strangest touch of all—the reflection of the face of Venus in the mirror held by the angelic Cupid. In the mirror she is a middle-aged woman, but in the flesh she is a young maiden. This *is* a mystery. Perhaps the message is that a woman can remain beautifully youthful even as she grows older. At least that is the message that appeals to me. In any case, the painting now means a great deal more to me than it did in the past, and it was my solitary contemplation that did it.

It is not too much to say that you have not experienced museum-going to the fullest if you have *never* been there alone. I commend it, even as an experiment. It puts one on one's mettle. It is *entirely* up to you how you spend your time, what you look at and what you pass by, how long you stand in front of a particular work, when you call it a day and end your visit. As I look back on the museum experiences that have made the most powerful impact on me, I know that there were certain works of art that spoke most directly to my heart because I was able to have a private communion with them.

COPING WITH CROWDS. It might be appropriate to close this chapter with a comment on the enormous crowds one often finds in museums these days. Of course, many great masterpieces can be enjoyed in relative solitude in the permanent collections of museums, but often one must contend with jam-packed galleries, trying to see what one can over the heads and under the arms of others. There certainly is a difference between the two experiences.

It is difficult to stand in front of an individual work for longer than a few seconds when people are milling around you, pushing and shoving to get on with the show. If you are especially moved by the works of art, you may be disturbed by the feeling that others have no sense of what you are experiencing. Kandinsky once wrote scornfully of "the vulgar herd" that strolls through museums and pronounces the pictures "nice" or "splendid." Then they go away, he added, "neither richer nor poorer than when they came."

Whenever you feel that way, do your best to shut out the sense of being with other people. It takes concentration, but it can be done. It helps when there are breathing spaces in the crowd, and for a minute or two you can be alone. It is wise to take advantage of these "gaps," moving across a room quickly and forgetting about seeing each work in sequence. There are also other tricks one can try, like going to a popular exhibition a half-hour before it closes, when attendance will have thinned out. But for the most part, crowds are a fact of museum life, and one must learn to live with them.

THE MUSEUM ITSELF AS A WORK OF ART

There are some museums in which the buildings and grounds are so spectacular that they dominate the collection. This is certainly true of Versailles, and Windsor Castle, and the Doge's Palace in Venice. One can even say the same of the much smaller Frick Collection in New York. Walking around and through such magnificent buildings, one is dazzled by every detail—doors, chandeliers, furniture, wallpaper, floors, fireplaces, ceilings, windows, roofs, gardens. One never knows what marvelous things there are to see in addition to the works of art on display. And in another way, the Centre Pompidou in Paris tends to upstage most exhibitions it presents.

What such experiences teach us is that almost every museum is worth looking at for itself. Surprising works turn up in unlikely places. In the St. Louis Art Museum in Missouri, for instance, there is the equestrian sculpture of the historic figure after whom the city was named, as well as one of Daniel Chester French's demure, bare-breasted maidens sitting in lovely splendor beside the main entranceway. In front of the Capitoline Museum in Rome, with its beautiful stairway, courtyard, and grand facade, all designed by Michelangelo, is the great *Marcus Aurelius* eques-

The Boboli Gardens, Florence

Overleaf left:
The Garden Court in the Frick Collection, New York

Overleaf right:
Charles Niehaus
Apotheosis of St. Louis.
c. 1906.
Pedestal: white granite, height 19′6″.
Figure: bronze, height 26′8″.
City of St. Louis, Missouri

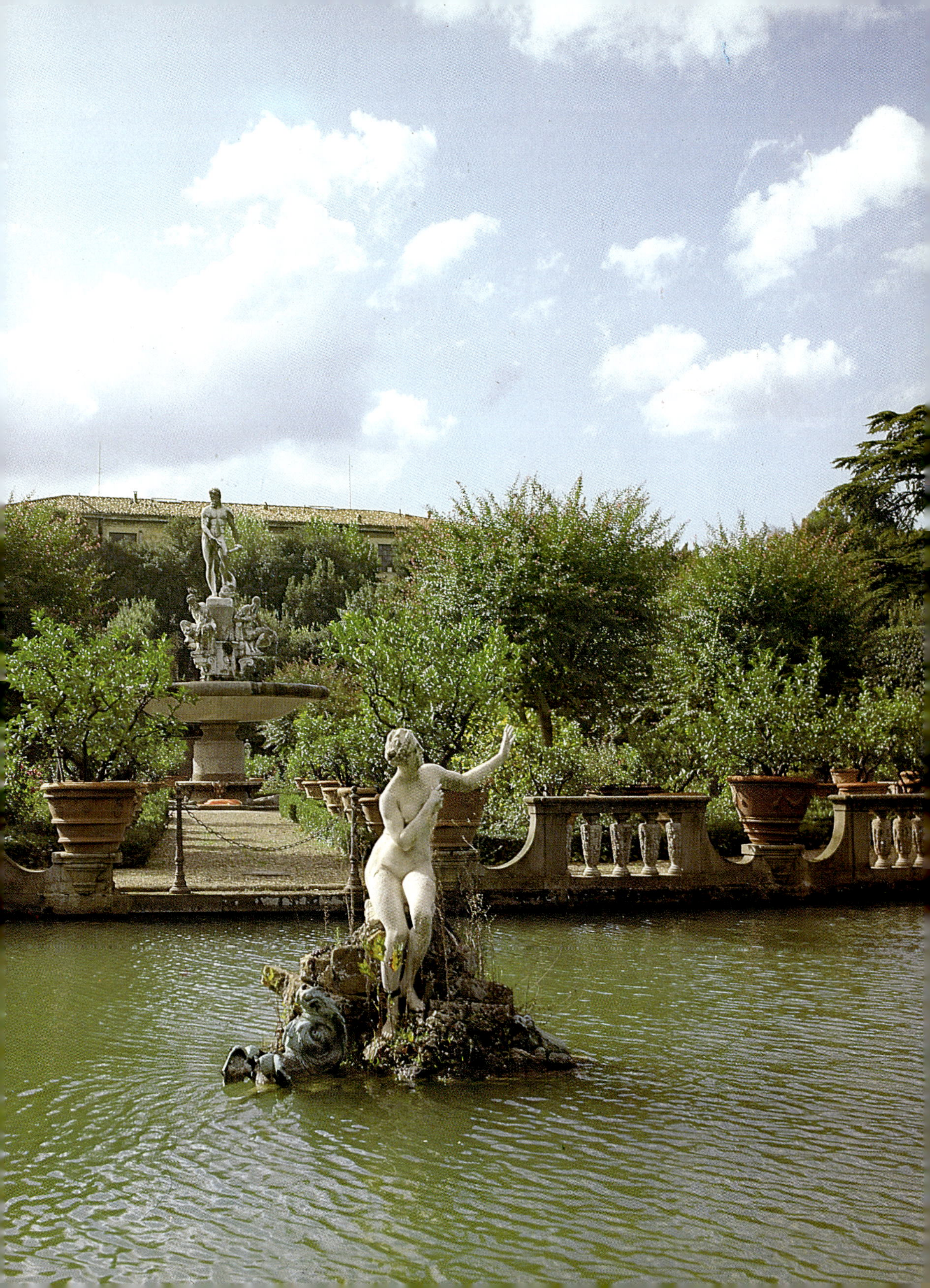

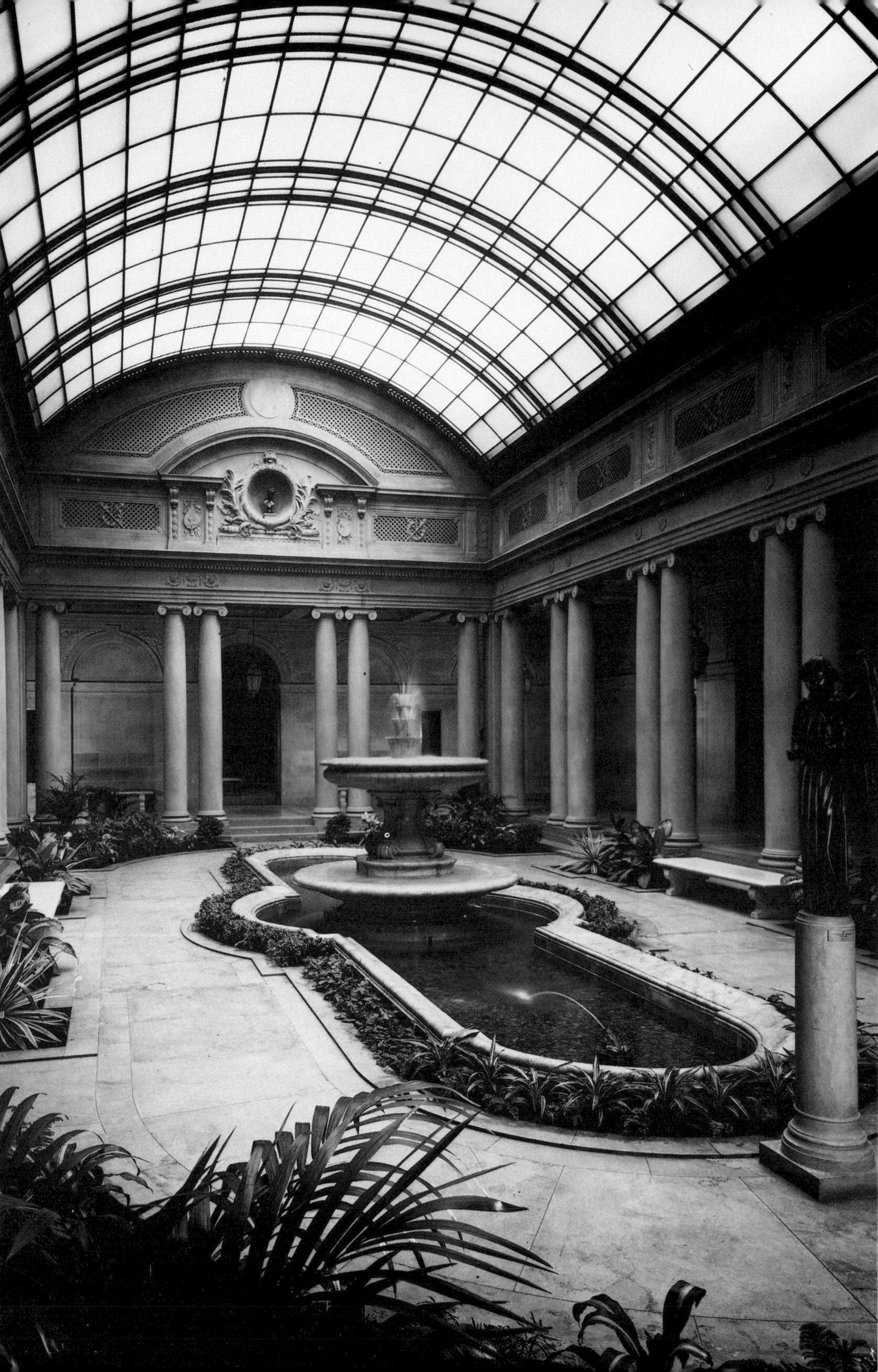

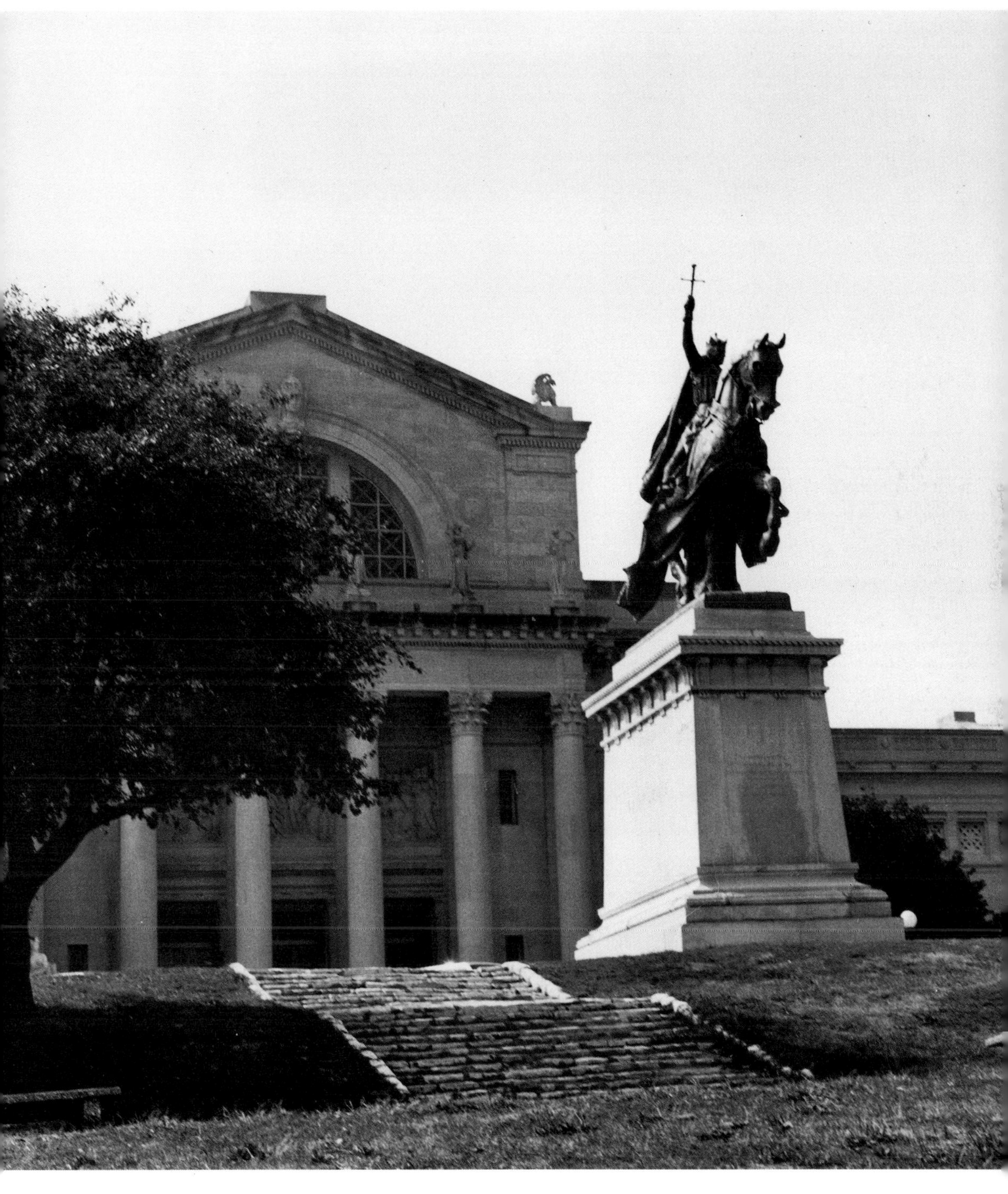

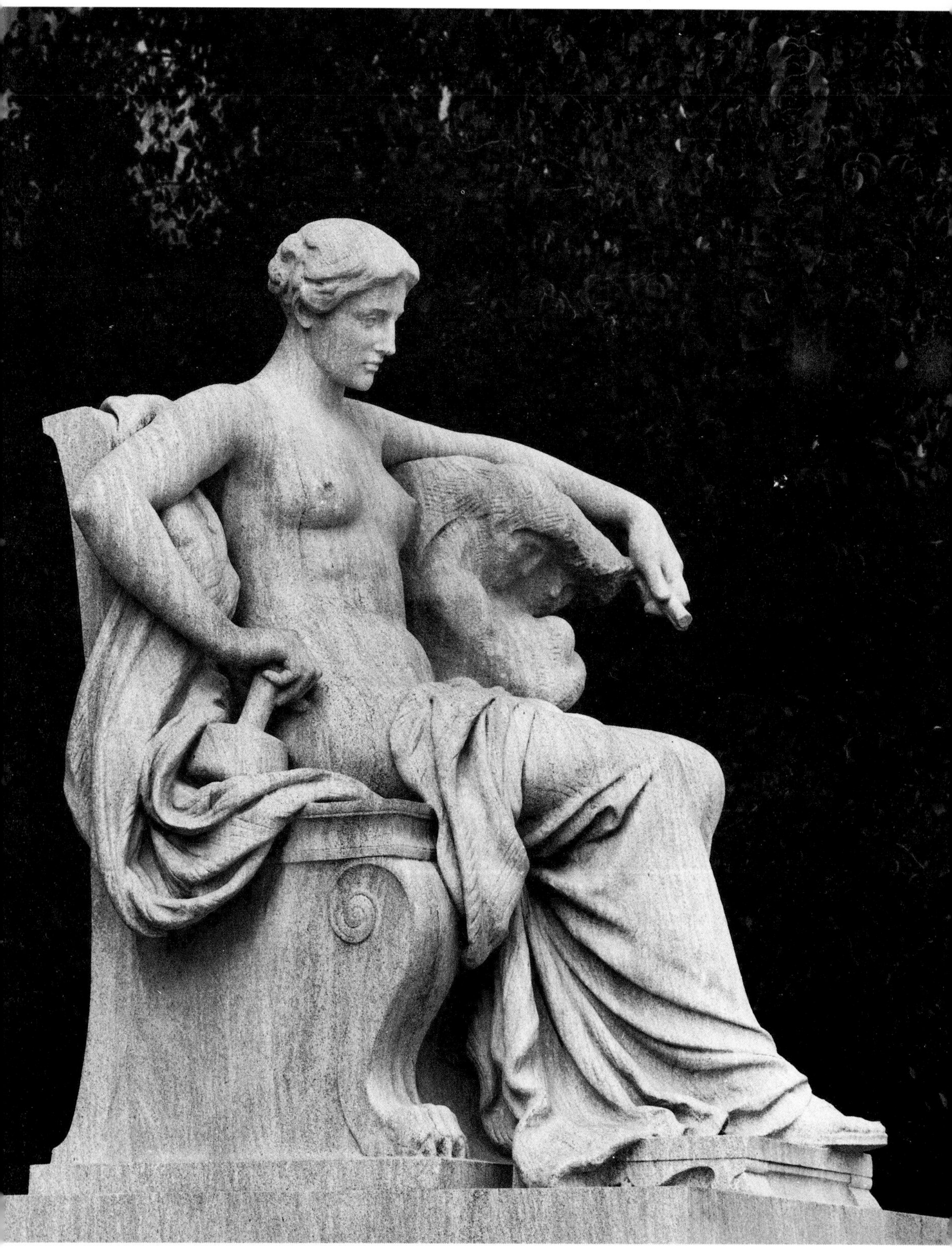

Daniel Chester French
Sculpture. c. 1900.
Knoxville marble,
height (with base) 9′1″.
The St. Louis Art Museum,
Missouri

trian monument. In front of the National Gallery of Modern Art in Rome—which is not one of the major tourist attractions of the city—there are fine sculptures by Jacques Lipchitz, Arnaldo Pomodoro, and others; and if one looks carefully at the building itself one can discover an interesting frieze that runs across the entire front. In London, the Tate Gallery sometimes has a lovely collection of Henry Moore sculptures on its front lawn. Over the doorway of the Victoria and Albert Museum there is a series of nineteenth-century rondels carved by Alfred Drury which contain some graceful figures accompanying what to me is an odd pronouncement by Sir Joshua Reynolds: "The excellence of any art must consist in the complete accomplishment of its purpose."

The stately classical columns of London's British Museum and New York's Metropolitan Museum of Art and the Brooklyn Museum, as well as the sculptures that are integrated into the architecture, are worth more than a fleeting glance as one approaches those buildings. A beautiful replica of Roman gardens is much to be enjoyed outside the J. Paul Getty Museum in Malibu, California. The extravagance of Renaissance gardens can still be seen in the Boboli Gardens in the rear of Florence's Pitti Palace, where sculptures and fountains in beautiful ponds and groves of trees make a summer's walk a rare delight. Not far away, in the Villa Demidoff, one can find an incredible giant sculpture by Giambologna hewn out of rock (or so it appears) in the midst of fields and forests. And the superb collection of Maillol and Rodin sculptures in the formal gardens in front of the Louvre, Cultural Minister André Malraux's gift to the people, make the approach to that museum a unique artistic experience.

Overleaf:
Alfred Drury
Rondels. 1906.
Victoria and Albert
Museum, London

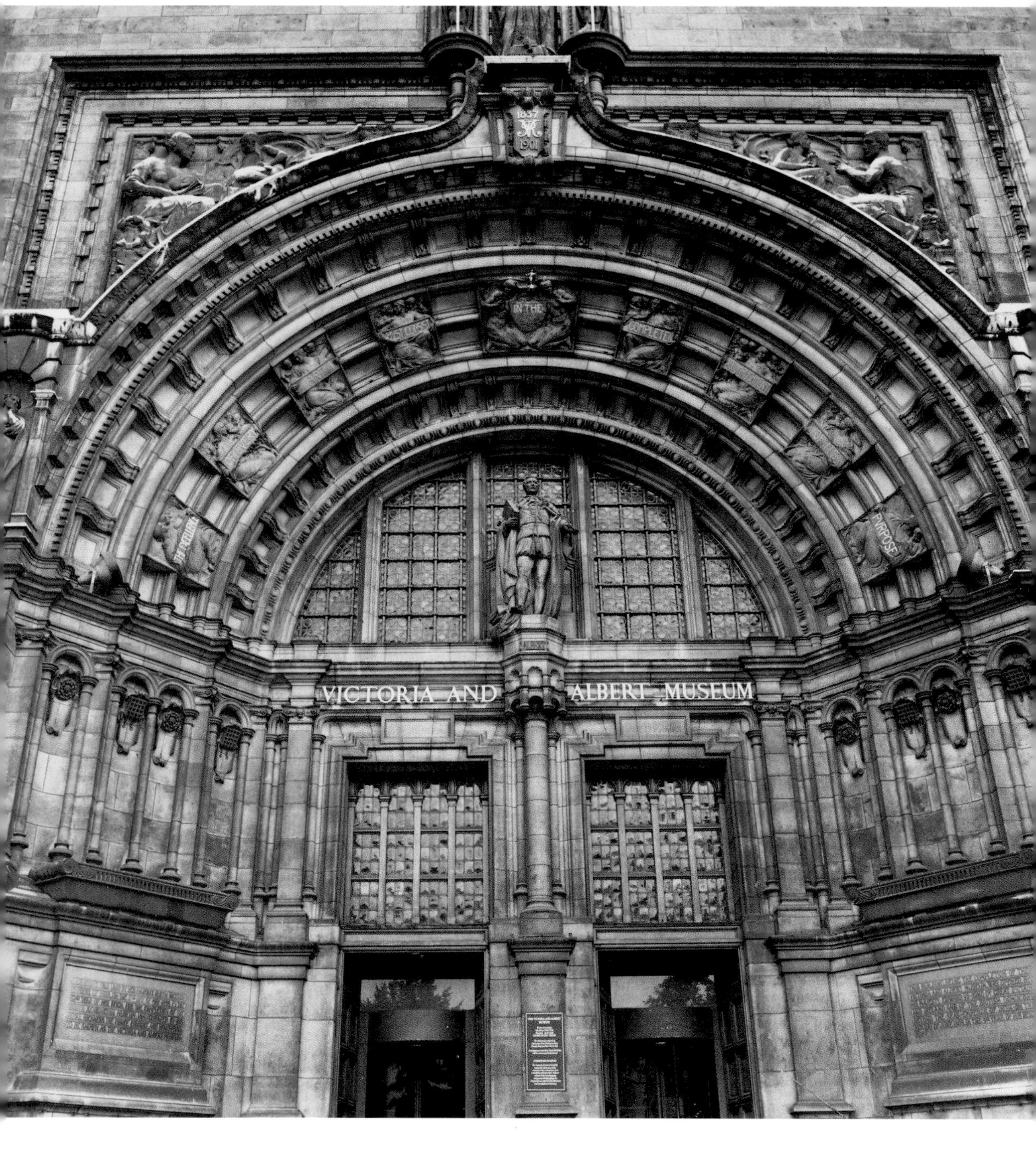
1837
1901
IN THE
COMPLETE
PURPOSE
VICTORIA AND ALBERT MUSEUM

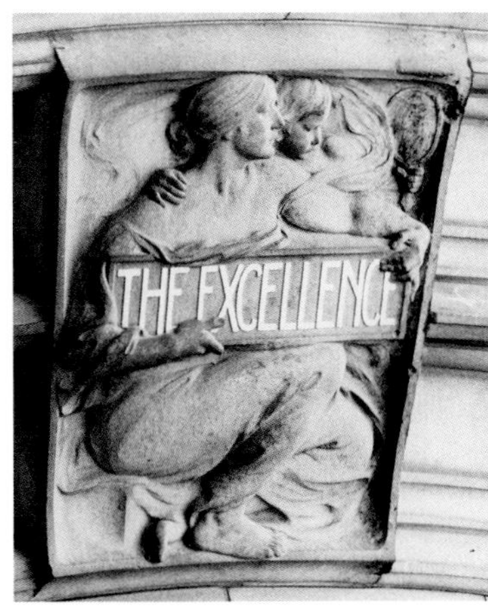
THE EXCELLENCE
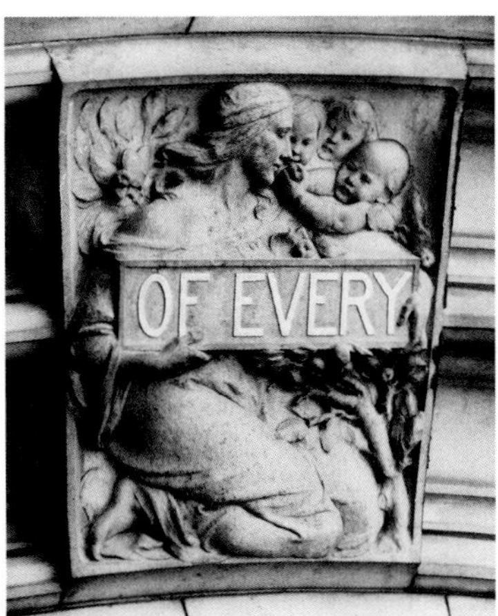
OF EVERY
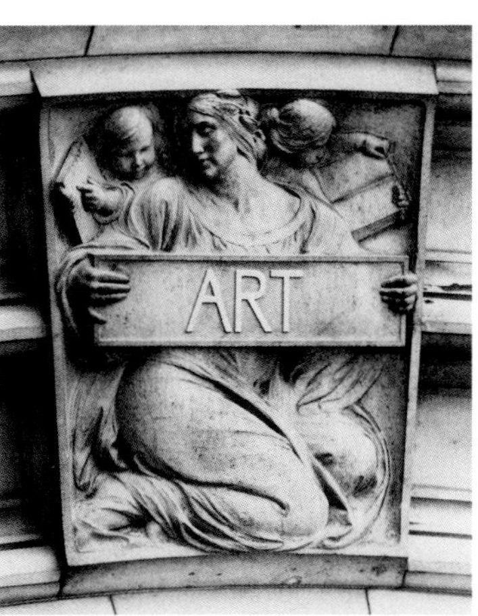
ART
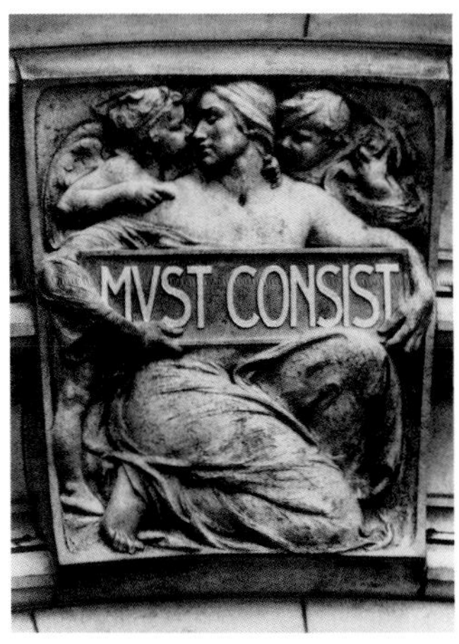
MVST CONSIST
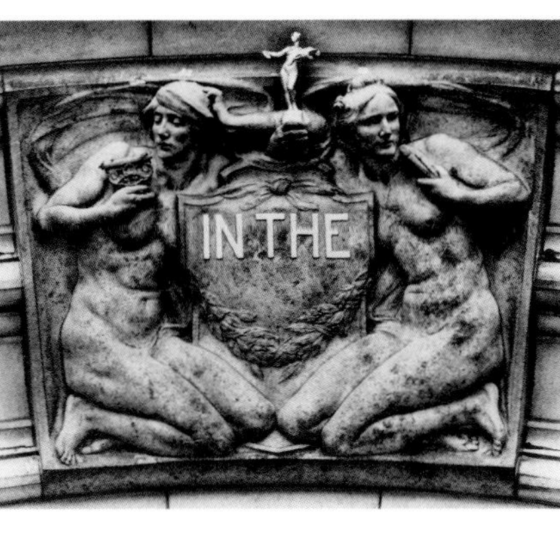
IN THE
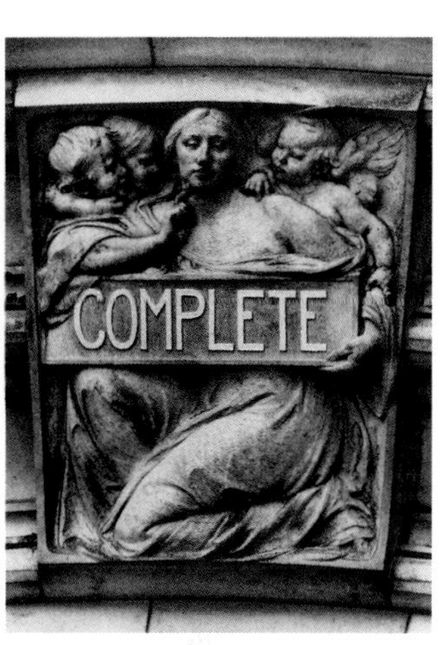
COMPLETE
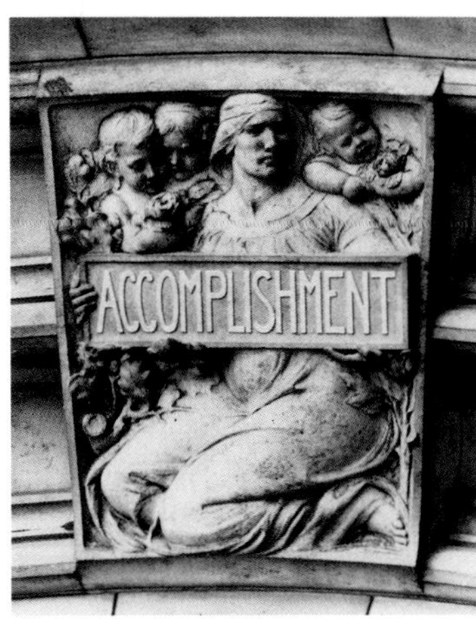
ACCOMPLISHMENT
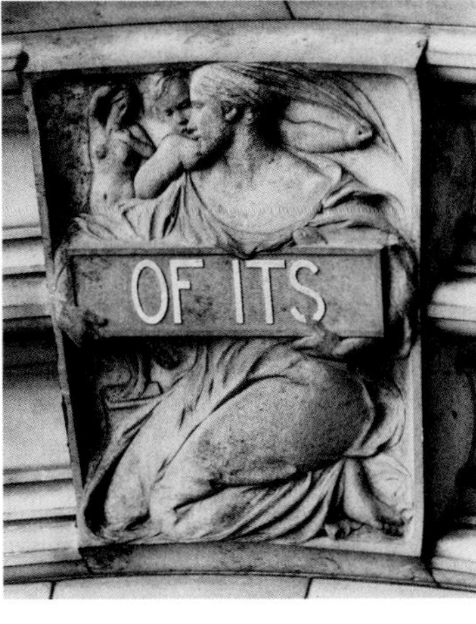
OF ITS
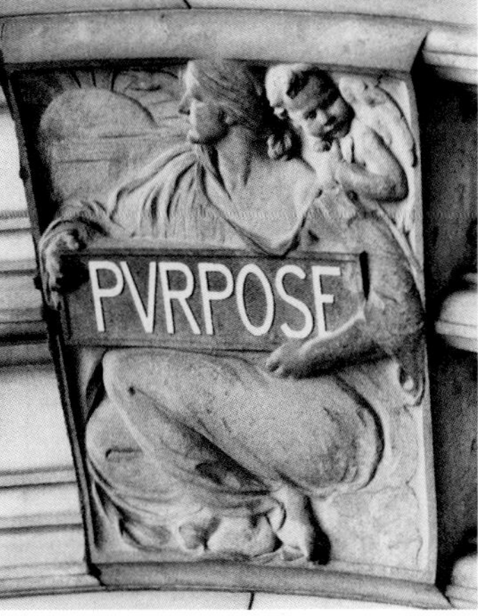
PVRPOSE

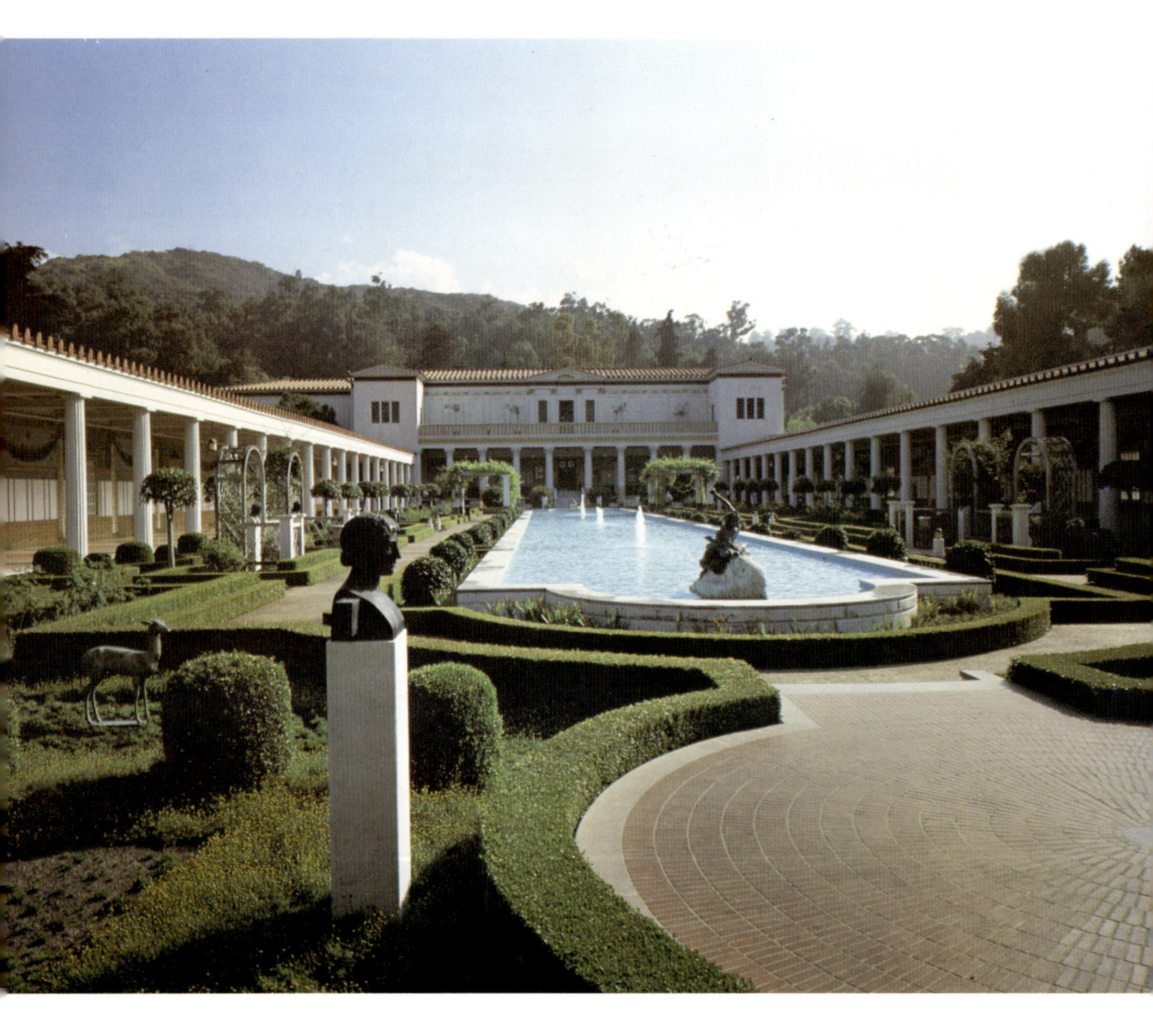

Peristyle Garden in the J. Paul Getty Museum, Malibu, California

In recent times, designing a museum has become a choice assignment for leading architects, their way of leaving their own artistic mark on the landscape. This is quite a departure from the eighteenth-century idea that museums should be designed for the sequential viewing of works of art. Today, museums have far more complex purposes. There are both permanent collections and special exhibitions to be visited. Museum shops feature postcard reproductions, slides, greeting cards, books, catalogues, replicas, jewelry, games, multiple works of art, and a miscellany of other objects. Restaurants help visitors enjoy a leisurely lunch during their museum visit. Lectures, films, and seminars are scheduled in attractive auditoriums. Children's sections feature educational programs. Large works of art adorn outdoor sculpture gardens. There are libraries, restoration studios, storage rooms, and no doubt many other facilities. The contemporary architect has to design a far more multipurpose building than did the architect a couple of hundred years ago when museums first came on the drawing boards.

Probably the most spectacular example of a museum that broke the pattern of the past is Frank Lloyd Wright's Solomon R. Guggenheim Museum in New York. There is certainly nothing like it in the world, and it has been the subject of controversy from the start. There are those who feel the building is an impossible space in which to show art on its long circular ramp, which resembles no other gallery that ever existed. It has even been said that Frank Lloyd Wright had no feeling for art and was not in the least concerned about designing a structure to show paintings and sculpture—that he wanted only to create a monument to his own genius.

Another school of thought, to which I belong, feels quite differently about the Guggenheim. I find the exterior design a delightfully unique form in its urban milieu, and I am constantly cheered when I enter the large atrium and see the lovely lines created by the ramps. The spaces seem ideal for exhibiting works of art; as you move from one intimate area to another, you can enjoy a few carefully hung or mounted works at a time without being overwhelmed by an indigestible mass. It is a museum in which you can spend a few minutes walking quickly through the exhibits or hours lingering over each work. Either way, you leave the museum with the sense of having had a rewarding experience of the works or exhibit.

Frank Lloyd Wright
The Solomon R. Guggenheim Museum, New York. 1957–59. Installation view of "Alexander Calder: A Retrospective Exhibition," 1964

Clearly, this is a matter of personal taste. Each of us may have favorite museums, and going there—almost regardless of what is being exhibited at the moment—is bound to be a pleasurable experience. Other museums are less satisfying, and we have to be prepared to overcome the architectural obstacles in order to enjoy the works of art in the collection.

MUSEUM MASTERPIECES. There are certain museums that I consider absolute gems, and I would recommend them unhesitatingly to museum-goers as ones that are most likely to have universal appeal. The Dumbarton Oaks Research Collection and Library in Washington, D.C., designed by Philip Johnson, is a fine example. An extraordinarily elegant structure, it helps one focus on beautiful objects in a most intimate and gracious setting. The Cleveland Museum of Art, with its striking black-and-white striped exterior reminiscent of the great cathedral in Siena, Italy, conveys a sense of excellence in every

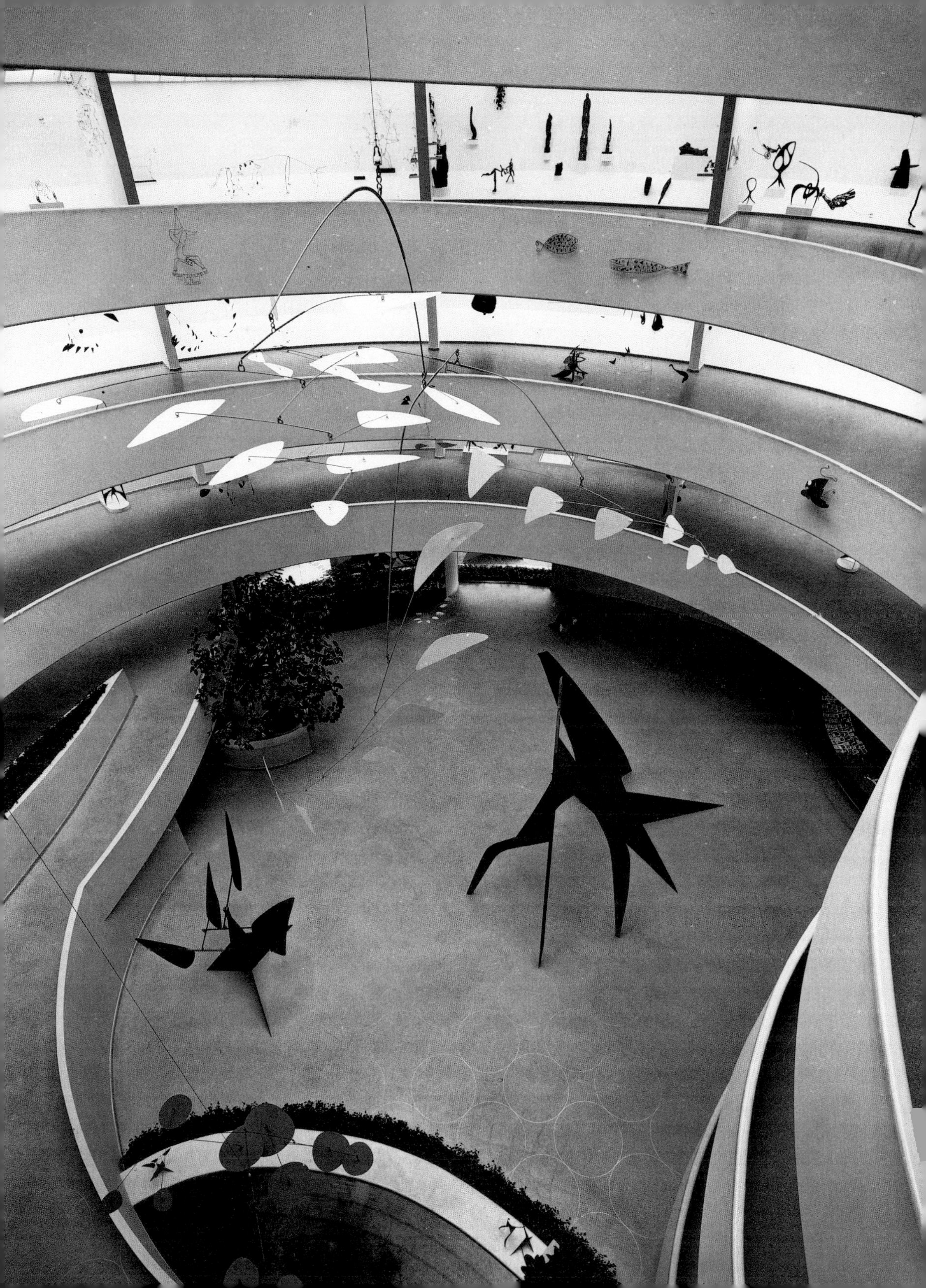

aspect. The Louisiana Museum of Modern Art is a wonderful museum just north of Copenhagen in Humlebaek which received its name because the man who made the initial gift of the land and house had been married three times, always to women named Louise. What is especially lovely about the Louisiana is its small and compact building, with skillfully designed galleries for viewing groups of sculptures and paintings. Outside the building is a landscaped area at the edge of the sea, with the Swedish coastline barely visible on the horizon. Sculptures are placed judiciously on the lawns, under trees, near rocks, and against the seascape, so that one can walk around the area and find an endless variety of lovely views.

An equally spectacular success in museum design is the Kröller-Müller State Museum located in a park in Otterlo, Holland. There, too, a small, compact building is ideally suited for the exhibition of paintings and sculpture, and there is a simply wonderful area outside with groves of trees, a beautiful lake, open spaces, wooded areas—all with sculpture extremely well placed in appropriate settings. A short walk from the museum building there is a clearing with three *Upright Motives* by Henry Moore mounted on an enormous pedestal made of differently shaped concrete blocks—which is itself a work of sculpture. The pedestal was designed by Moore from fragments that were originally intended for the foundation of a much larger museum building that was to be erected on the spot. The money for the larger building never materialized—to the delight of those who think the smaller building is ideal—and Moore decided to use the blocks in the pedestal for his sculpture. He has said that one of the marks of a good site for sculpture is whether people like to have

Louisiana Museum of Modern Art, Humlebaek, Denmark.
View of museum grounds.
Sculpture: Henry Moore. *Two-Piece Reclining Figure 5*. 1963–64. Bronze, length 12′3″

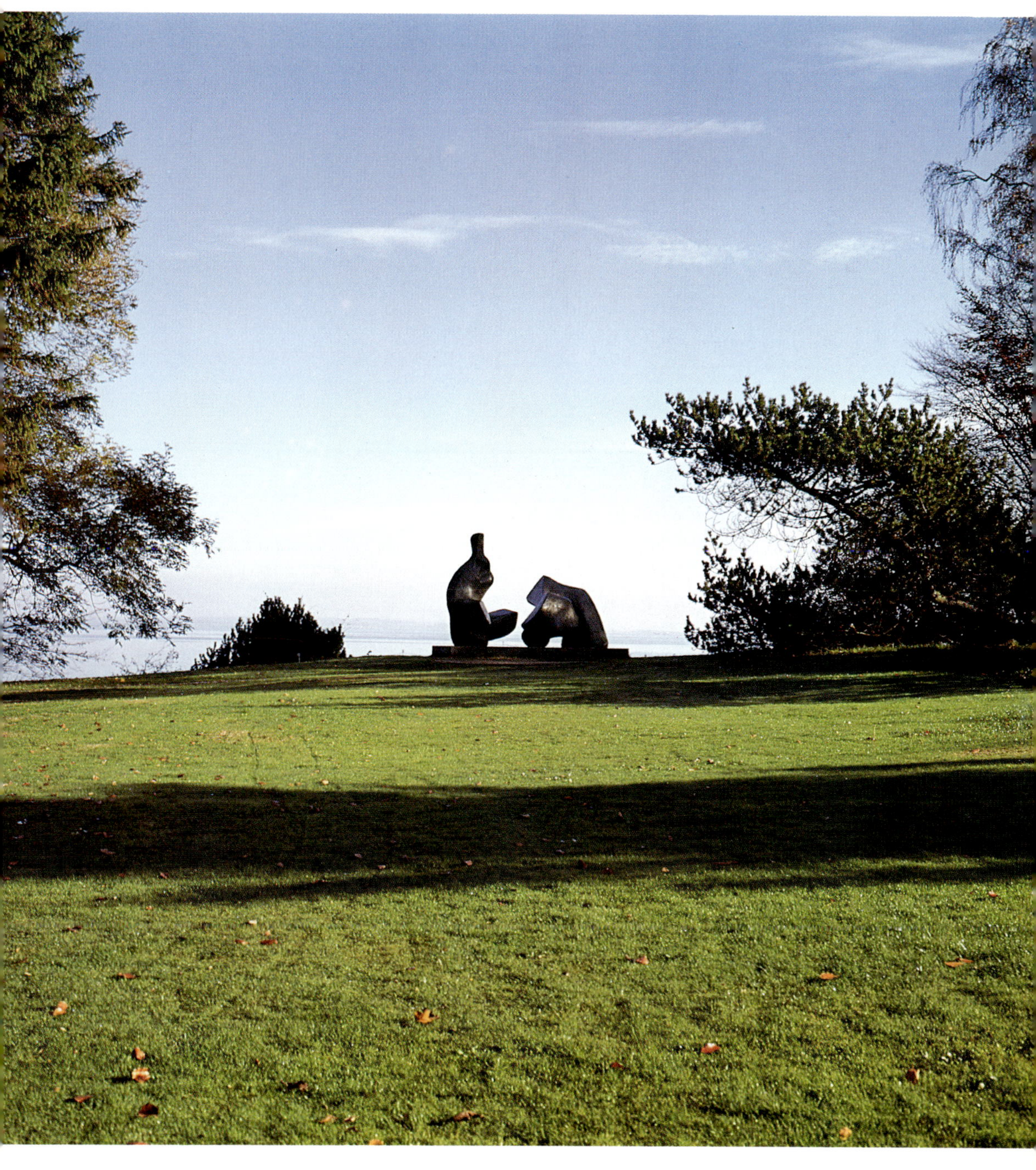

their picture taken in front of it, and by that definition the three *Upright Motives* in the Kröller-Müller should win some kind of prize.

Alberto Giacometti
Standing Figures.
Bronze, height 3′ to 5′.
Louisiana Museum of Modern Art, Humlebaek, Denmark

PRIVATE COLLECTIONS. Museums situated in what were stately homes have a different type of attraction. Certainly one of the most beautiful in that category is the Frick Collection in New York, which possesses not only some of the greatest masterpieces of Western art but shows them in a most luxurious and restful setting. And it is always a pleasure to linger around the indoor pool in the center of the building, or to sit down for a few minutes and imagine what it is like to live in a magnificent home.

Something of the same experience can be felt in the Pierpont Morgan Library, which is housed in another splendid New York home and has small, exquisite exhibitions of manuscripts and drawings. Then, there is the Isabella Stewart Gardner Museum in Boston; the du Pont family collection in Winterthur, Delaware; the Ringling Museum of Art in Sarasota, Florida; the Hearst collection in San Simeon, California; the Huntington Library and Art Gallery in San Marino, California; the Marion Koogler McNay Art Institute in San Antonio, Texas. European counterparts include the Wallace Collection and the Courtauld Institute Galleries in London, the Horne Museum in Florence, the Burrell Collection in Glasgow. Each one of these includes supreme masterpieces which one can experience as if they were still part of a great private collection.

Some of the great homes in England that have been turned into museums, like Chatsworth, Woburn

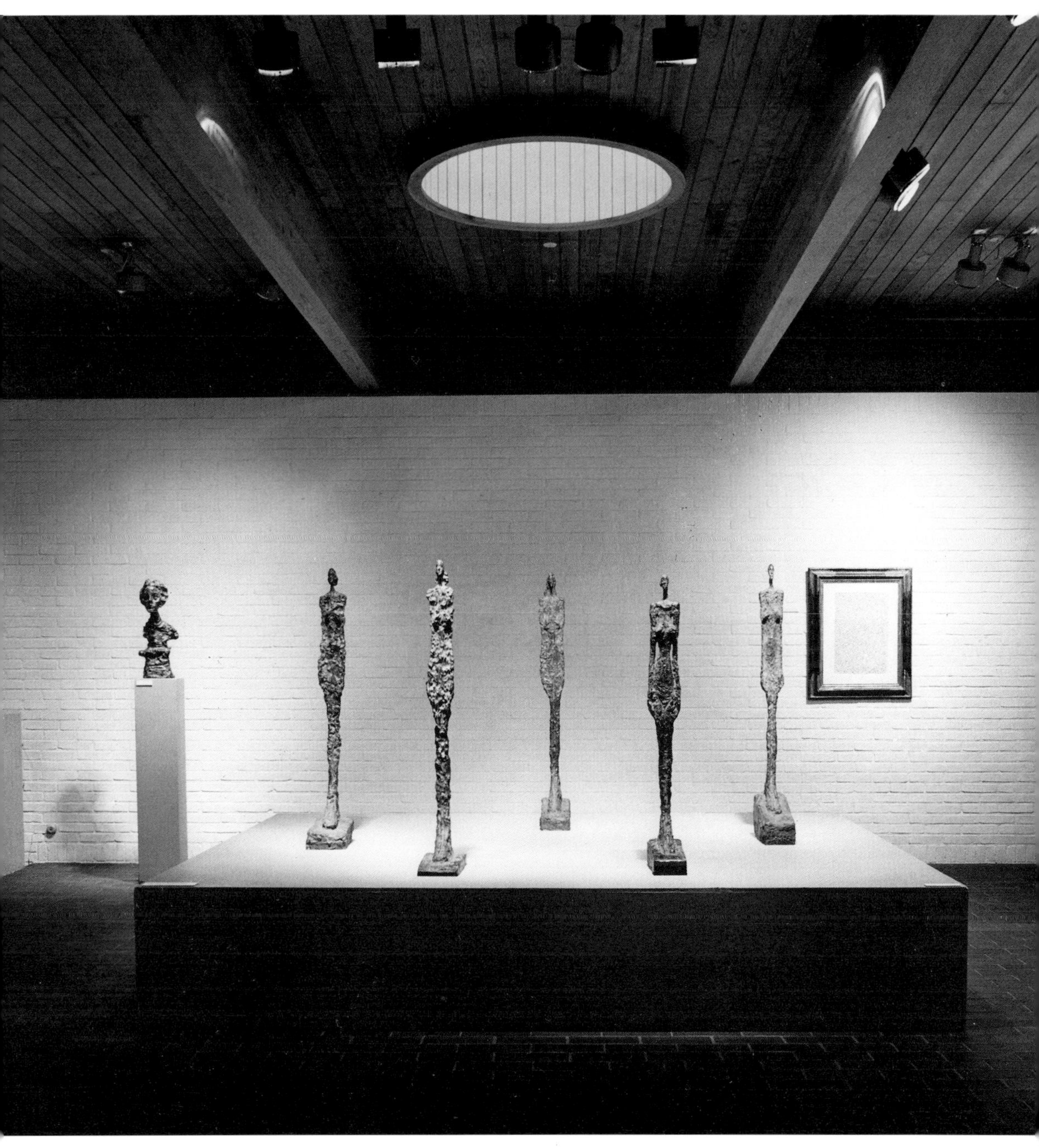

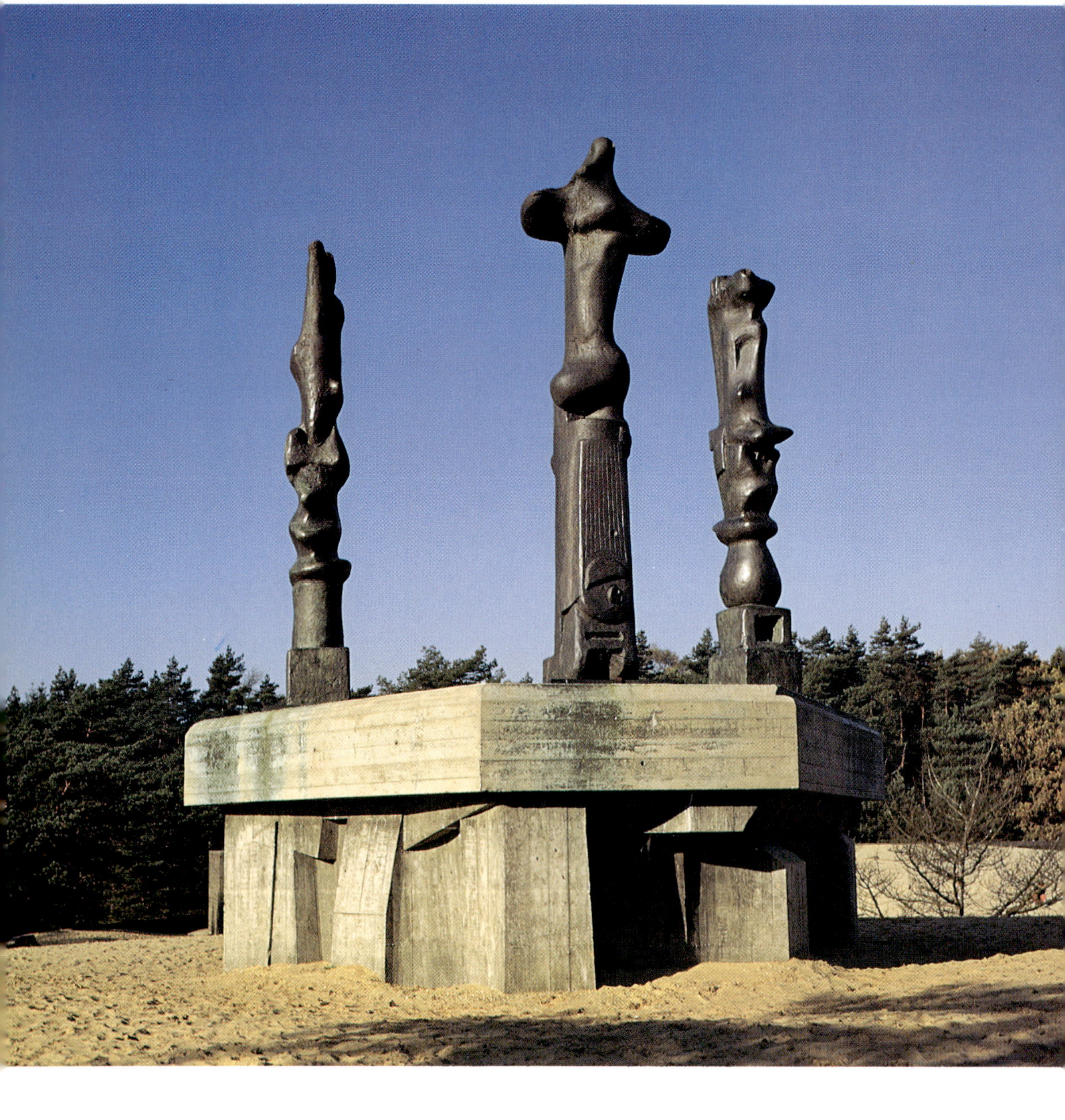

Henry Moore
Upright Motives 1, 2, 7.
1955–56.
Bronze, height 11′;
length 10′6″; width 12′6″.
Kröller-Müller State
Museum, Otterlo, the
Netherlands

Below: Detail

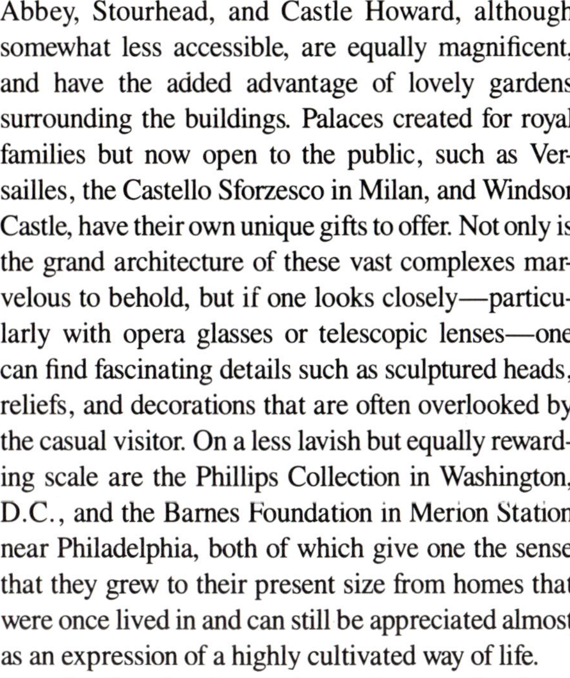

Abbey, Stourhead, and Castle Howard, although somewhat less accessible, are equally magnificent, and have the added advantage of lovely gardens surrounding the buildings. Palaces created for royal families but now open to the public, such as Versailles, the Castello Sforzesco in Milan, and Windsor Castle, have their own unique gifts to offer. Not only is the grand architecture of these vast complexes marvelous to behold, but if one looks closely—particularly with opera glasses or telescopic lenses—one can find fascinating details such as sculptured heads, reliefs, and decorations that are often overlooked by the casual visitor. On a less lavish but equally rewarding scale are the Phillips Collection in Washington, D.C., and the Barnes Foundation in Merion Station near Philadelphia, both of which give one the sense that they grew to their present size from homes that were once lived in and can still be appreciated almost as an expression of a highly cultivated way of life.

Another development over the years has been the university museum. Oxford has its Ashmolean Museum, and Cambridge its Fitzwilliam Museum. Harvard has the Fogg and Busch-Riesinger museums. There are fine museums at Yale, Princeton, Brown, UCLA, Berkeley, the State University at Purchase, New York, and dozens of other campuses around the country.

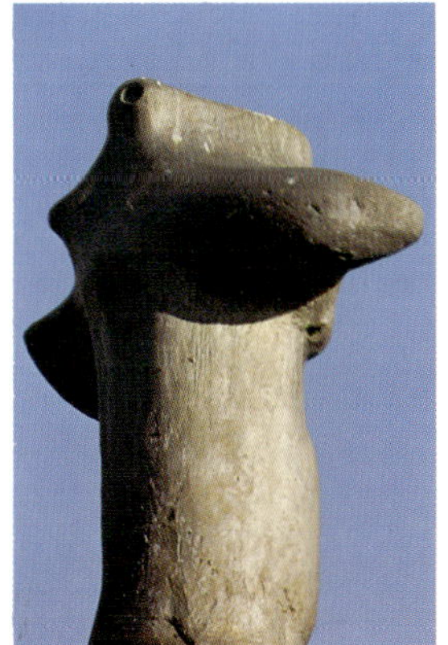

THE NEW ARCHITECTURE. Some of the famous museums built in recent times help develop an appreciation of contemporary architecture when one makes a visit. Receiving a museum commission has, in fact, become a much cherished prize for

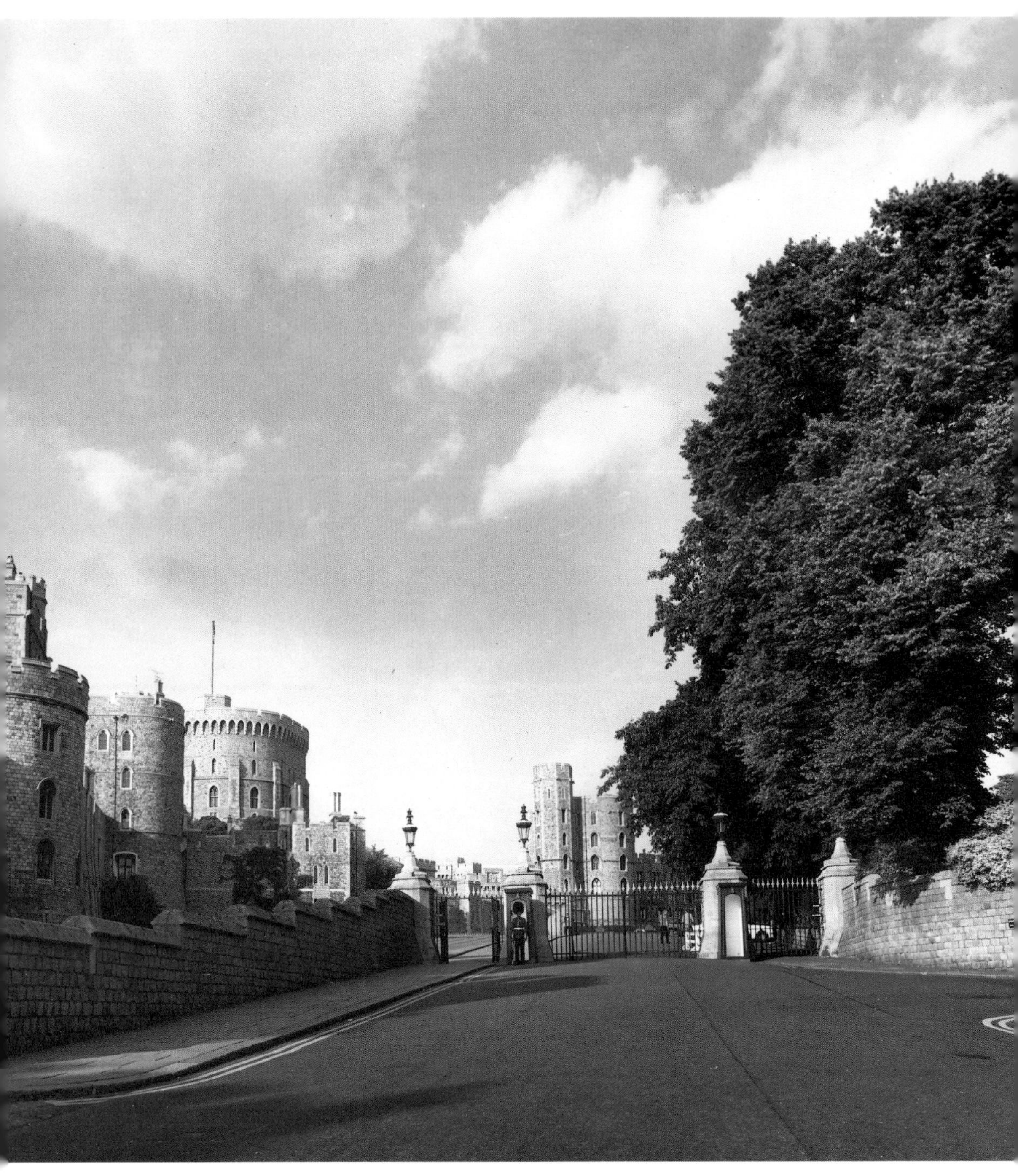

contemporary architects, an opportunity to show one's most creative resources. Some of the finest buildings of the past few decades have been museums designed by Philip Johnson, I. M. Pei, Gordon Bunshaft, Richard Meier, Edward Larrabee Barnes, Marcel Breuer, Louis Kahn, and many other outstanding architects of our time. New museum buildings have been springing up in dozens if not hundreds of cities around the world. I have already mentioned the Guggenheim as being one such museum. Another architecturally historic example is the East Building of the National Gallery of Art in Washington, D.C., designed by I. M. Pei to create remarkable shapes in the air, like a giant piece of sculpture. As you approach the entranceway, the grand sloping forms of an enormous Henry Moore sculpture, *Knife Edge Mirror Two Piece,* offer a most rewarding beginning to your museum visit. Inside, a monumental Calder mobile rotates slowly against the skylight in an enormous space that constitutes the main area of the museum. There are corner spaces and balconies and walkways here and there on which choice works of art are displayed. It is an experience just to be there and look around for a few minutes, to enjoy the remarkable integration of different art forms.

The West Wing of the Museum of Fine Arts, Boston, also designed by I. M. Pei, is equally beautiful as a building. The dramatic architectural element is a glass vault that rises above the public space of the museum to provide a place where people walk, sit and talk, eat, and shop. The Crystal Palace effect of the Galleria and the finely cut ashlar masonry walls provide an esthetic experience worthy of an outstanding museum. But once again the exhibition spaces in this wing are unimpressive. They consist of simple,

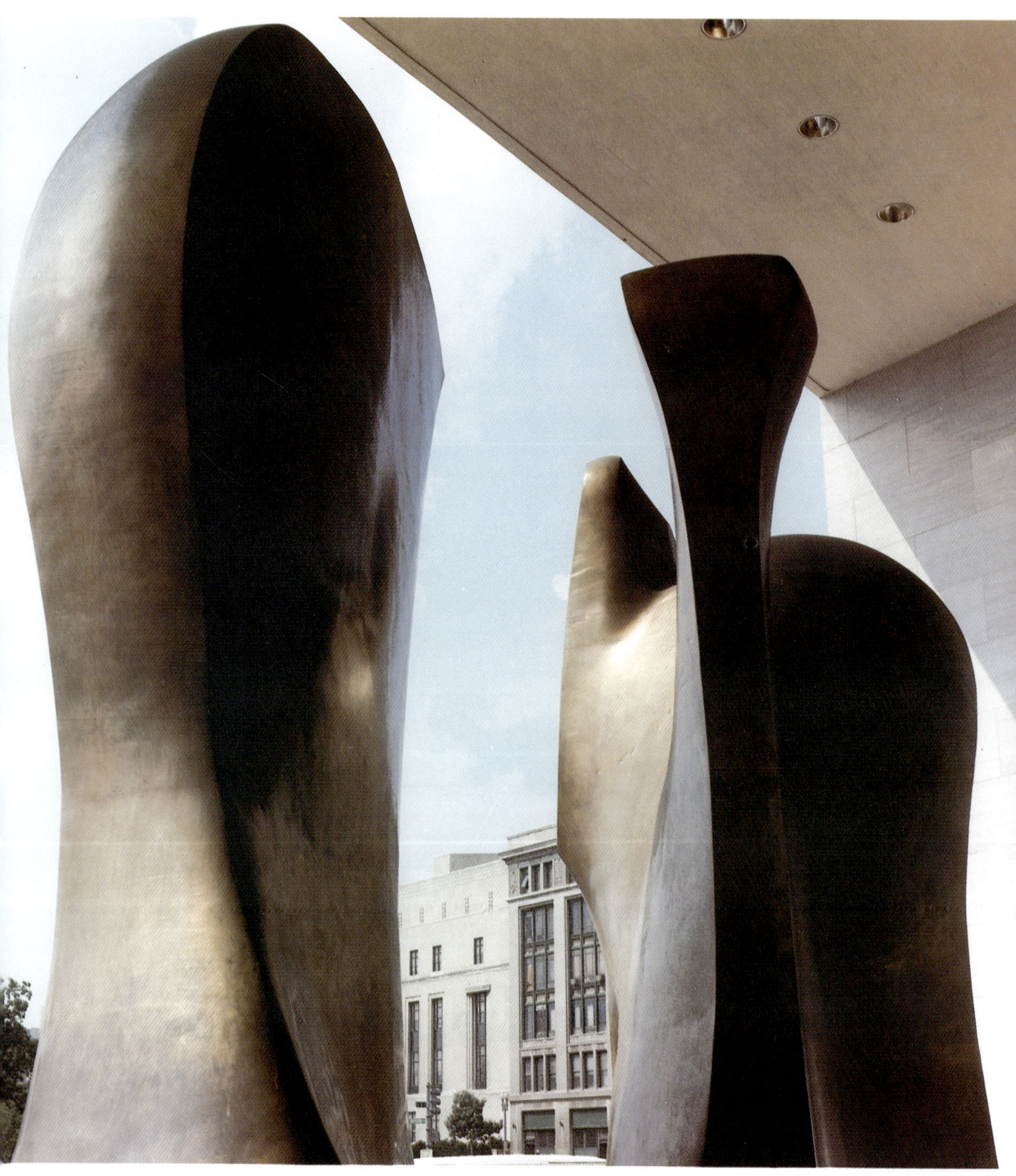

Henry Moore
Knife Edge Mirror Two Piece. 1977–78.
Bronze, length 25′.
National Gallery of Art, Washington, D.C.
Gift of the Morris and Gwendolyn Cafritz Foundation, 1978

enclosed galleries where one examines the paintings or sculpture without any regard to the architecture. There seems to be a message in the design. It says: "By all means come to the new wing to see the exhibition on hand, but also use the museum as a meeting place, plan to spend time in the restaurant and shop in order to get the most out of your visit."

The Hirshhorn Museum, in Washington, D.C., was designed by Gordon Bunshaft. Its controversial exterior doughnut shape suffers by comparison with the National Gallery's East Building. But once inside, the visitor is invited to look at art rather than the building. That is one's only purpose for being there, and the museum has been designed to make that process as effective and meaningful as possible. Each floor has two rings of galleries: an inside ring that faces a glass wall to provide natural daylight for viewing sculpture, and an outside ring that consists of enclosed spaces for the exhibition of paintings. There are connecting openings between the two rings, and one is invited to go back and forth from sculpture to paintings at will. By the time you have finished going through the galleries, you will probably feel that the museum has served its main purpose very well. The outdoor sculpture areas in the center of the atrium and around the base of the building also work well enough, although one could wish for more greenery to soften the stark environment.

The new building for the Museum of Modern Art in New York has won almost universal praise for its grand spaces and beautifully presented sculpture garden. And new museums in Dallas, Atlanta, Fort Lauderdale, and other cities in the United States and around the world show that the trend to create museum showplaces is, if anything, on the increase.

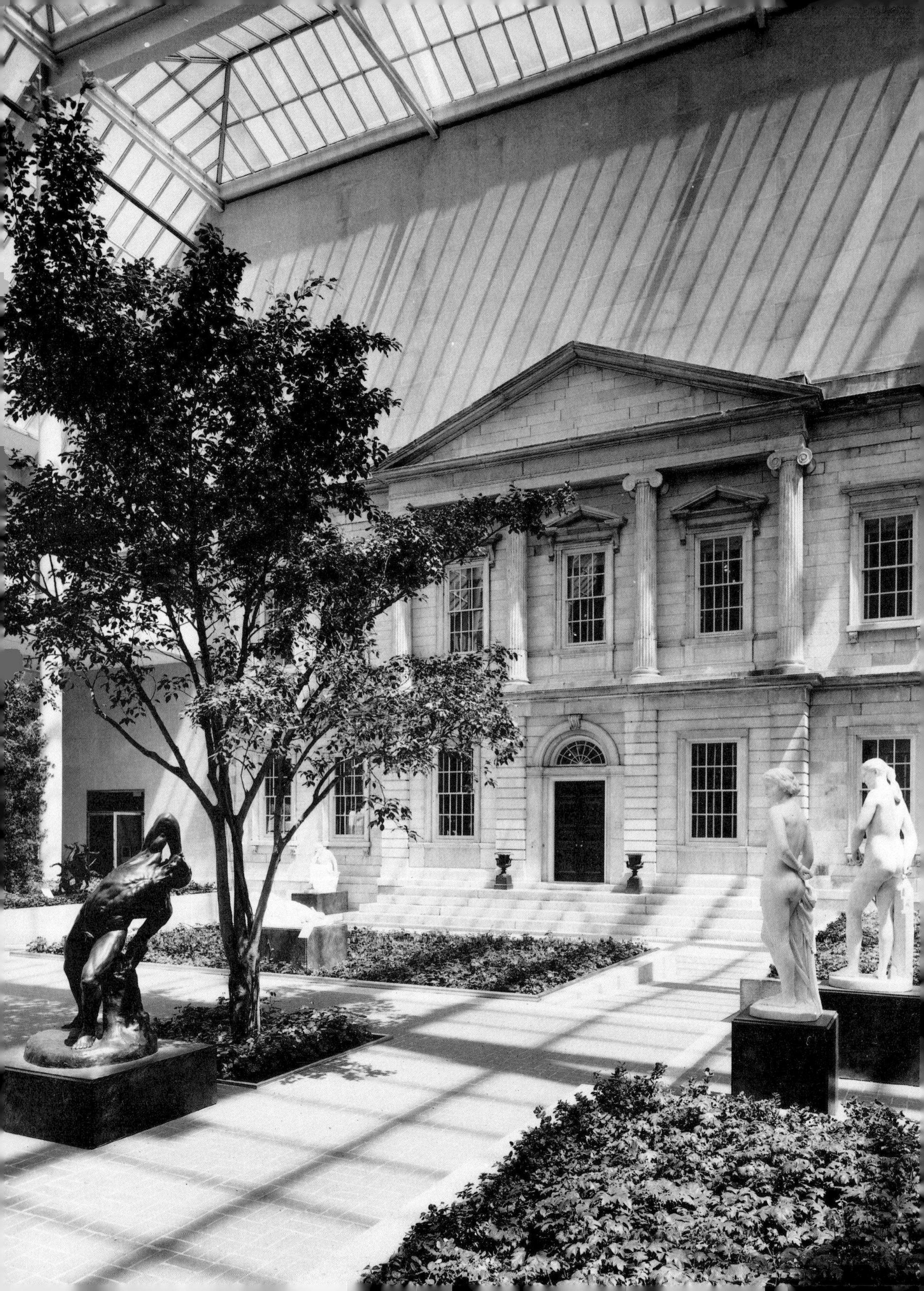

Kevin Roche, John Dinkeloo & Associates
The American Wing, the Metropolitan Museum of Art, New York.
Exterior view

ENCYCLOPEDIC MUSEUMS. Visiting the Metropolitan Museum of Art in New York, which is the most encyclopedic museum in the world, creates quite another reaction. A good case can be made that the formidable size of the Metropolitan makes it unworkable as a single museum. No visitor could possibly endure to visit all its richly endowed wings in one day: its collection of Renaissance paintings, the nineteenth-century André Meyer Wing, the Lehman Collection, the medieval rooms, the photography department, European decorative arts, the Michael Rockefeller Wing of primitive art, the Greek and Roman, Oriental and Far Eastern, and Egyptian collections, the American Wing, the collection of twentieth-century art—to say nothing of its Arthur Sackler Wing and the special exhibitions that are always a major attraction. Any one of these departments could be a major museum in its own right, demanding hours to look through carefully.

In a 1982 exhibition on "New American Art Museums," the American Wing of the Metropolitan Museum, designed by Kevin Roche, John Dinkeloo and Associates, was singled out as one of the "more conspicuous examples of the greenhouse aesthetic." It is a delight to see, both inside and out, providing one with the experience of being in an outdoor garden inside the museum. The wing where the Lehman Collection is housed also has its own distinctive architectural character, and when the Henry Moore exhibition was held there in 1983, its vaulting spaces provided a unique setting for his sculpture. The Michael Rockefeller Wing is still another architectural achievement, which makes the viewing of this superb collection of primitive art a special plea-

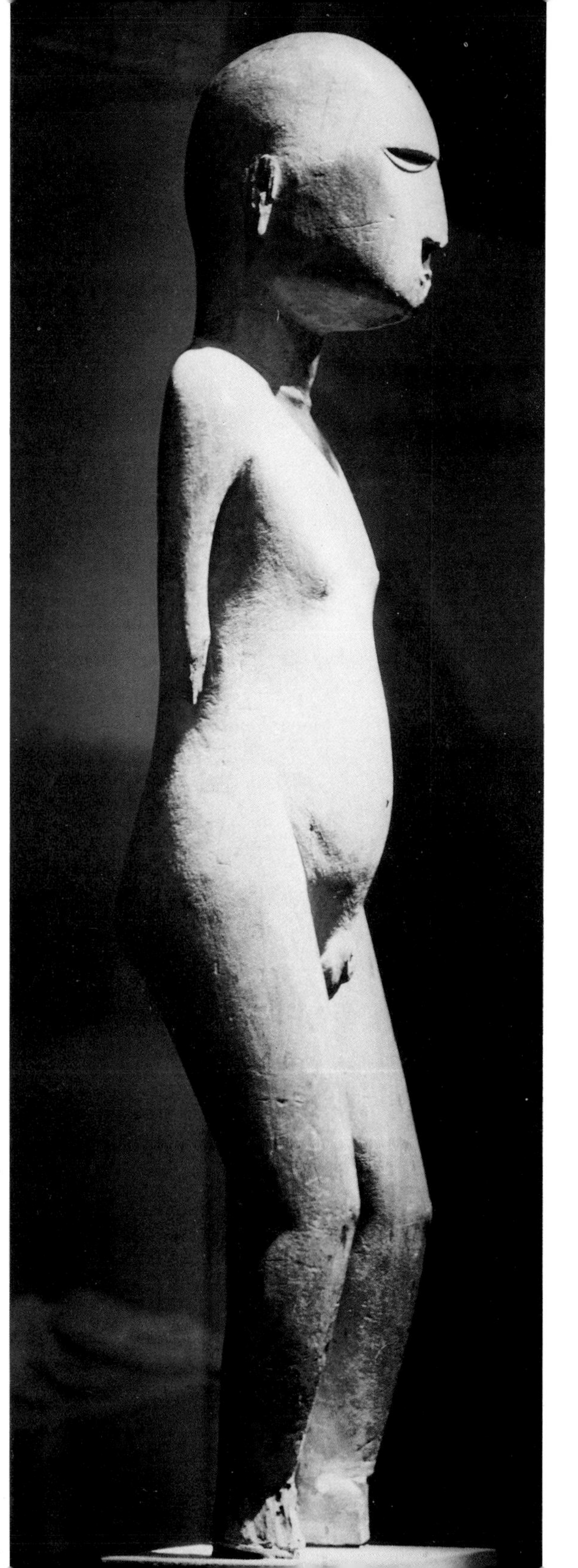

Standing God
Late 18th century.
Wood, height 33¾″.
Gambier Islands, Polynesia.
The Michael Rockefeller Wing, the Metropolitan Museum of Art, New York

Right: Detail

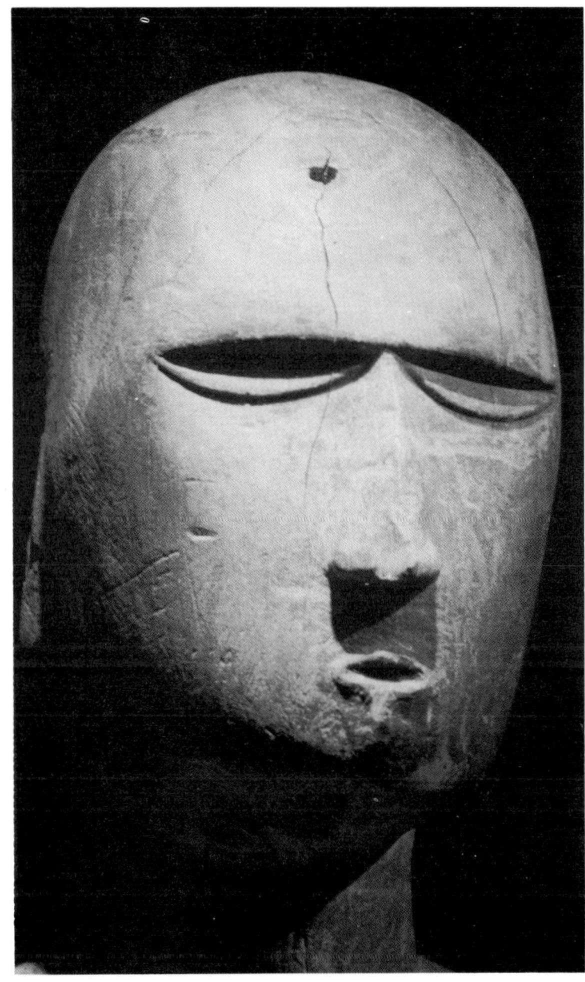

sure. One can make trips to the Metropolitan just to see one or another of these collections, leaving the rest for other trips. Planning one's visits on such a piecemeal basis, if at all possible, is undoubtedly the best way to enjoy this unique institution.

The same can be said for the other great

museums that have grown too vast over the years. On entering the Louvre one feels that it is more than ever the palace it was in the past. Its grand spaces create a sense of awe by their very size and elegance. The same is true of the Hermitage Museum in Leningrad, whose labyrinthine character gives one the same sense of hopelessness one feels when trying to see everything at the Metropolitan or the Louvre in one visit.

NOT TO BE OVERLOOKED. Something should be said about museums that house great collections but do not display them dramatically. The National Museum in Athens is laid out in such a way that you cannot tell which objects the museum curators consider to be its artistic treasures and which are there because of their archaeological or historical significance. To someone accustomed to having museum curators draw attention to the most important items in their collection, this can be disconcerting. We do not expect to have to make discoveries by ourselves in great museums, though it may seem perfectly natural in an antique shop. It is always a revelation to see works borrowed from a small museum one has visited in the past and find them highlighted in a spectacular way as part of an exhibition in a major museum. It reminds one to keep the eyes and mind open and to try not to be put off by installations or architectural environments that seem less than spectacular.

The opposite side of this coin is the museum that invites you to fall in love with a field of art with which you were quite unfamiliar. For instance, there is no better place to get acquainted with the splendors of pre-Columbian art than the National Museum of Anthropology in Mexico City. The gigantic Olmec stone heads seem as at home here as they did in their natural environment.

Sometimes a fabulous museum, either in design or reputation, is so overwhelming that one risks overlooking a fine collection in a less well-known museum nearby. A visitor to New York may not realize that the Frick, the Whitney, the Guggenheim, and the Metropolitan museums are all within a short walking distance of each other. In Washington, D.C., the National Gallery and the Hirshhorn are close neighbors. In many large European cities there are clusters of museums in certain sections of the city. And do not be misled by some of the more forbidding names of museums. In Istanbul, for instance, the Tokapi Museum is on every tourist's list as a "must," but few visitors realize that the Archaeological Museum nearby has some extraordinary treasures, including the famous so-called *Alexander Sarcophagus*.

MUSEUMS FOR INDIVIDUAL ARTISTS. Some of the most surprising discoveries can be made in a museum that displays the works of a single artist in the place where the artist lived or worked. In such museums the environment helps one understand the kind of person the artist was and the influences that affected his work. Once, almost by accident, I came across a museum in Paris devoted to the work of Jean-Jacques Henner, whom I had never heard of before. His paintings have a marvelous rich glow, and I became a devotee of his work as I walked from room to room in what obviously had been his

Overleaf:
Gustave Vigeland
The Wheel of Life. 1934.
Bronze, diameter 9′10″.
The Vigeland Sculpture Park, Oslo

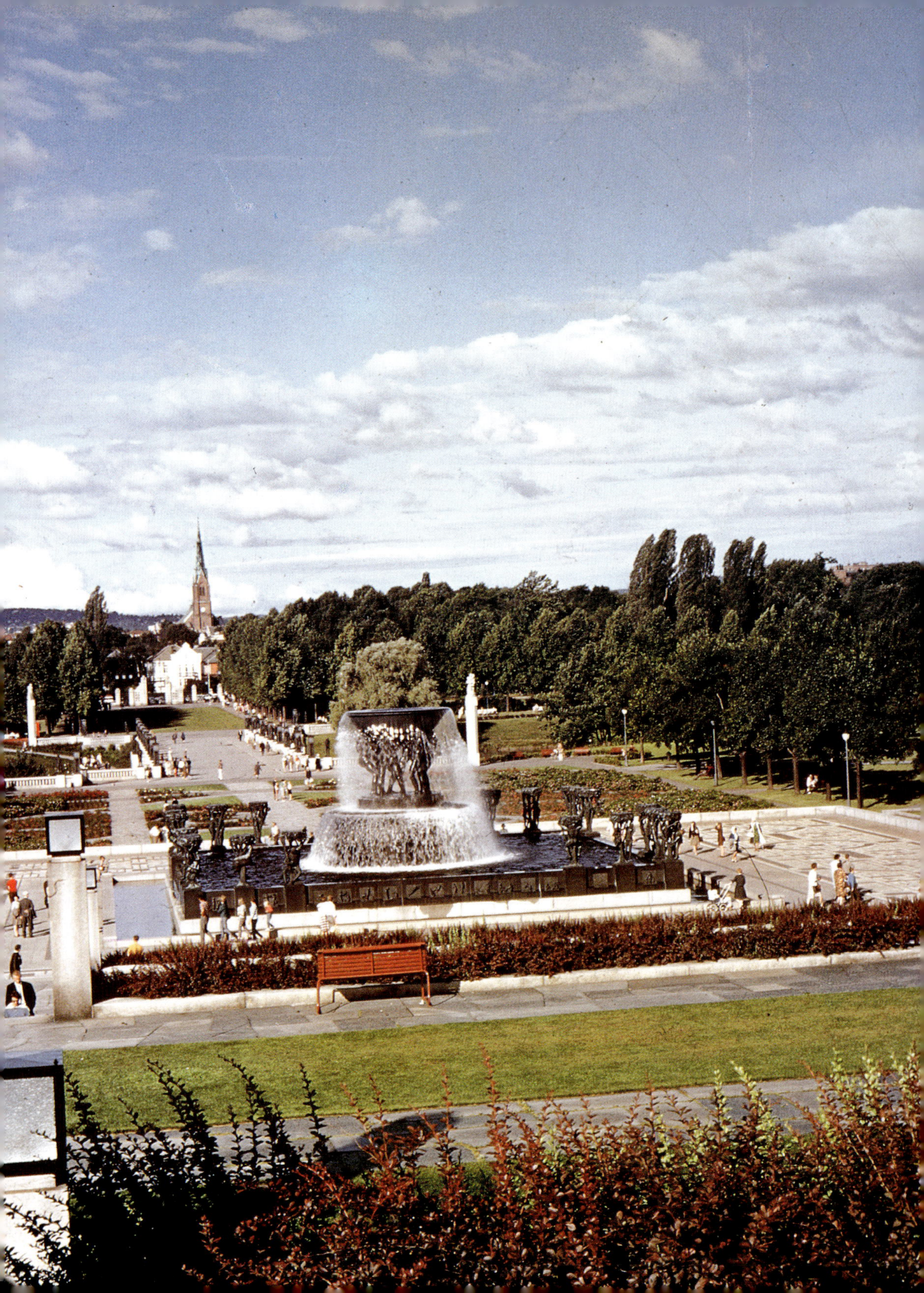

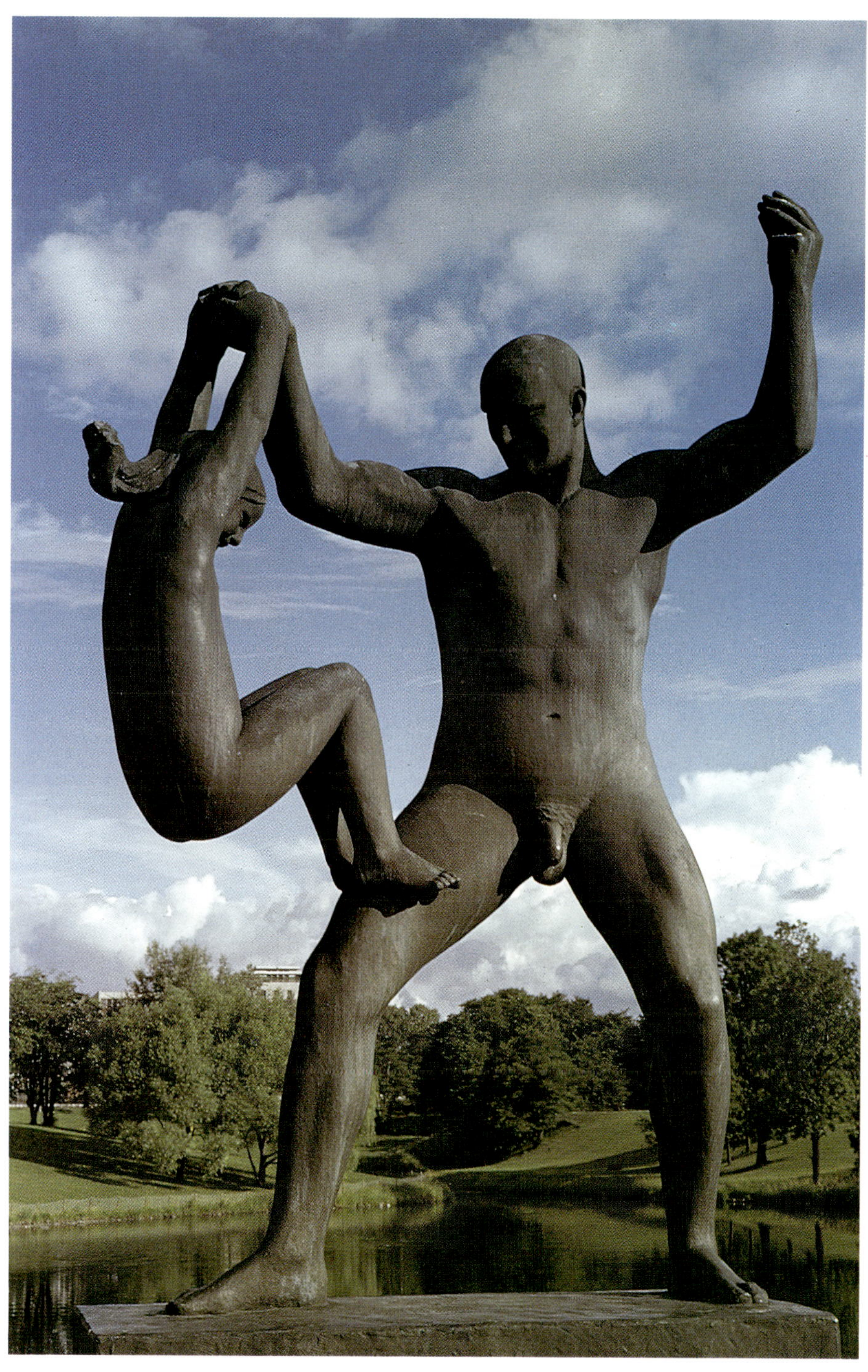

home. I have always enjoyed the work of Gustave Moreau, but I was stunned by the range of his work when I visited the Moreau Museum in Paris. Henry Moore has willed his home in Much Hadham, England, to the nation so that people will be able to see the studio in which he worked, the countryside that was a source of inspiration to him, and a selection of his sculpture.

Alexander Calder
The Arch.
Steel painted black, height 56′.
Storm King Art Center, Mountainville, New York

In the early years of the twentieth century, the sculptor Gustav Vigeland made a contract with the city of Oslo: the city provided him a studio for the duration of his life and Frogner Park in which he could place his sculptures. In return, he promised to devote himself exclusively to creating sculptures for the park. Over the years, Vigeland produced what he called *The Cycle of Life,* the story of human relationships from infancy to old age. There are hundreds of sculptures in Frogner Park, showing mothers and fathers with children and grandchildren, lovers of all ages in every conceivable relationship with each other—some tender, some wild, some angry, some passionate. There are bronze sculptures, stone carvings, and a monolith filled with writhing figures. An indoor museum houses a collection of his plasters. There are many of these special museums scattered around the globe, where one can see an artist's work in his home environment.

The experience is quite different when one visits a major museum that has been established for the purpose of showing the work of a single artist. The Rodin Museum in Paris is a wonderful place in which to view Rodin's works. The same is true of the Rodin Museum in Philadelphia, the Vincent van Gogh Museum in Amsterdam, the Thorvaldsen Museum in Copenhagen, the Munch Museum in Oslo, the

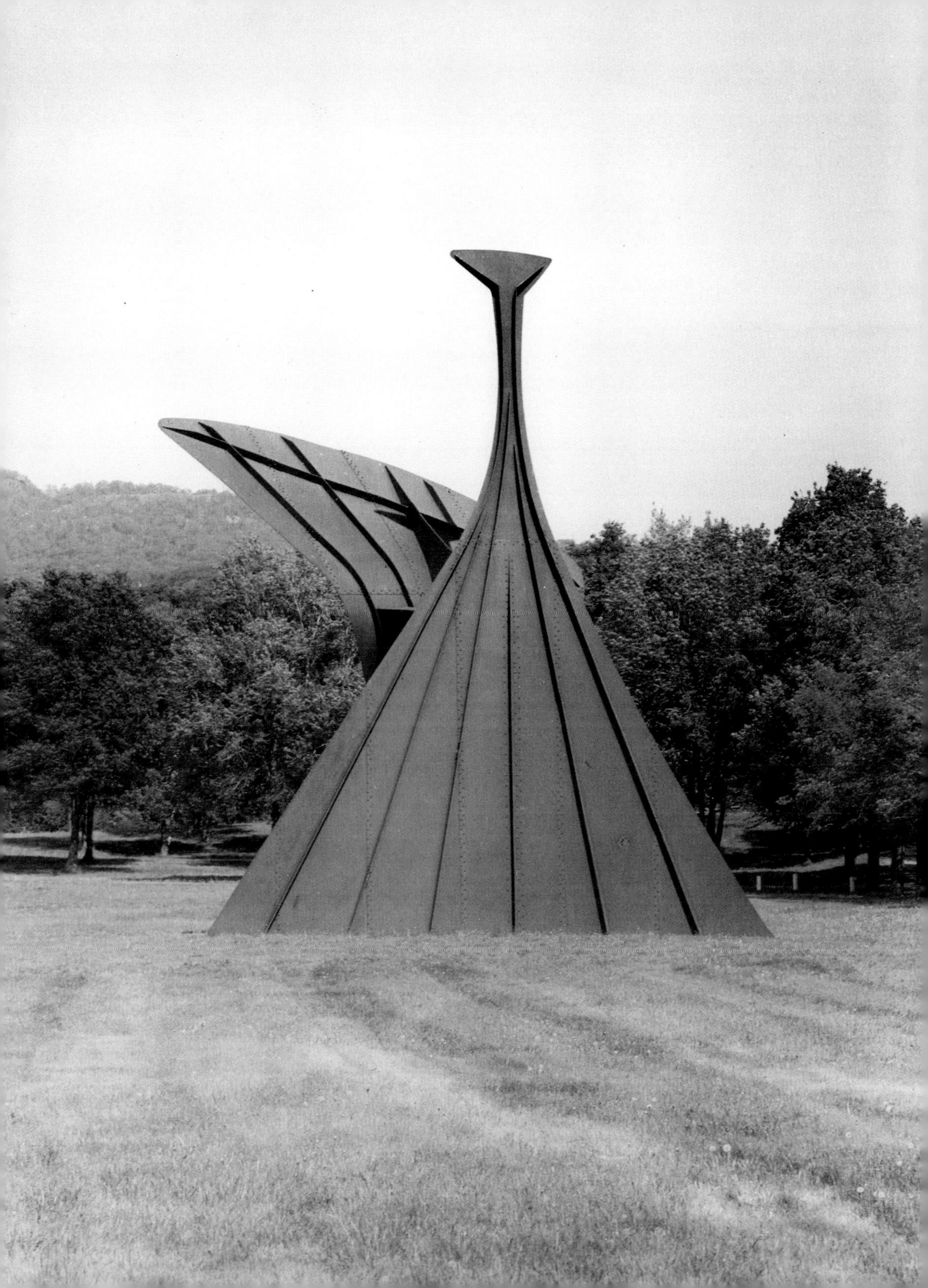

Wilhelm-Lehmbruck-Museum in Duisburg, Germany, the Marc Chagall Museum in Nice. Here representative collections have been assembled and housed in structures that seem particularly appropriate to an overview of the artist's work.

Giambologna
Apennine. c. 1580.
Stucco, brick, and stone, colossal size.
Villa Demidoff, Florence

OUTDOOR MUSEUMS. Finally, when one thinks of museums as works of art, one must touch on outdoor museums. Seeing sculpture in the open air is not a new idea. Ancient monuments in China, Cambodia, India, Egypt, Greece, to say nothing of more remote places like Easter Island, attest to man's desire to see sculpture against the sky. The great lions on the Greek island of Delos are among the most powerful of all outdoor sculptures.

The J. Paul Getty Museum in Malibu, California, re-creates what Roman sculpture gardens were like. Renaissance sculpture gardens were perhaps even grander, judging by the Boboli Gardens in Florence and the Villa Demidoff in Pratolino. Outdoor sculpture also has its place in Versailles, Paris, Vienna, and many other great cities of the world. In the sixteenth century, an outdoor sculpture park was created in Bomarzo, Italy, just north of Rome, and visitors can still see its gigantic sculptures of ogres, giants, monsters, mythological figures, animals, and monumental fountains placed dramatically in the midst of a relatively wild landscape.

One of the most beautiful of modern sculpture gardens is the Storm King Art Center in Mountainville, New York, where contemporary sculptures are placed with the utmost care and discretion on two hundred acres of magnificent rolling country. Walking around the grounds is a wonderful way to spend a

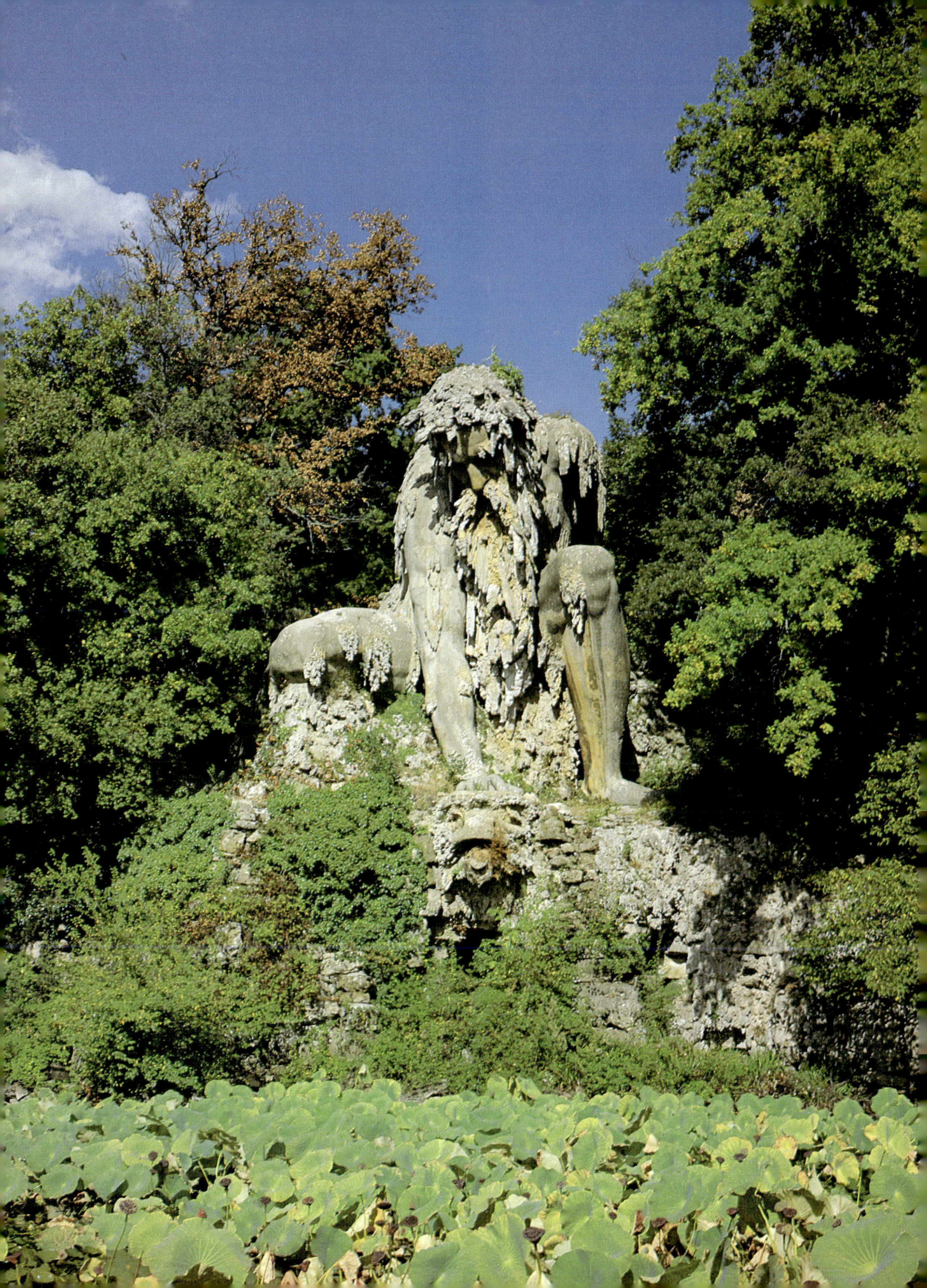

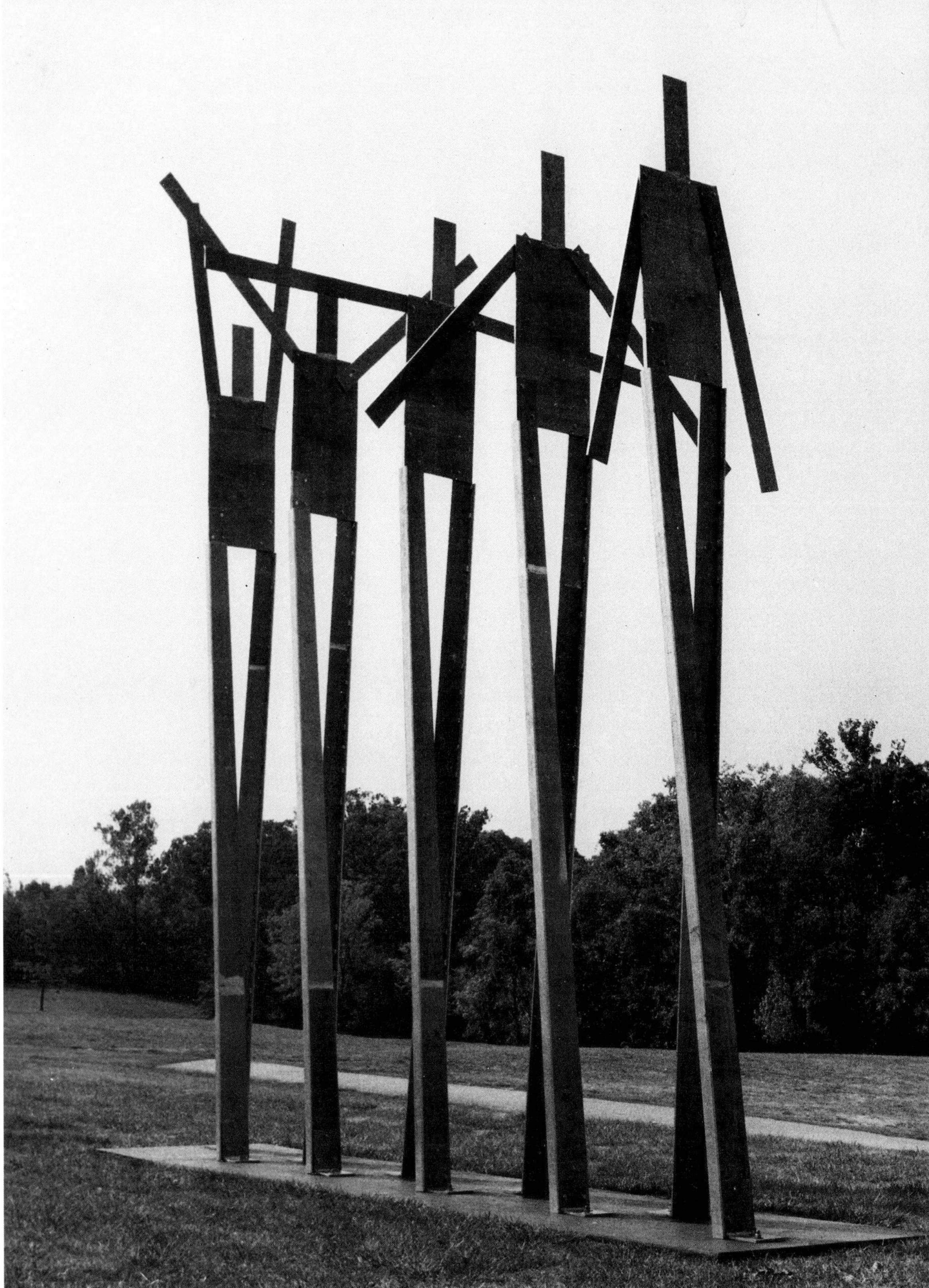

William King
Everything. 1982.
Aluminum, height 26′.
Laumeier International
Sculpture Park,
St. Louis, Missouri

summer afternoon. A more recent and also lovely sculpture park is Laumeier International Sculpture Park in St. Louis, which seems to be following the Storm King model of careful placement. Still another approach is found in Brookgreen Gardens in Murrells Inlet, South Carolina, where figurative sculpture is beautifully sited in a carefully designed landscape.

Many museums around the world are establishing special areas in the grounds outside their buildings for the exhibition of sculpture. It is always worthwhile to set aside some time to walk through those areas, and to sit down and enjoy great works of art in pleasing natural surroundings.

Describing a museum that is a work of art is no easier than describing any other work of art. But if you are prepared to look at the architecture and the environment as well as the specific objects in a museum, then just being there, looking into unexpected places, and discovering beautiful things will bring you great rewards.

WHERE AND WHEN TO GO

Most people visit museums when they travel to a distant city or country that is known for its cultural treasures, or when they want to see a special exhibition that has just opened in a local museum, or when they decide to revisit a favorite museum to look at works of art they have not seen for a while. Each of these involves different kinds of experiences.

You do not *have* to spend time in museums on your first visit to London, Paris, Rome, or Tokyo, but since you are reading this book, you probably will want to. One problem will be to decide which museum or museums to visit in the time you have available. The first and most important step is to identify the major museums in the city, to find out what the collections consist of, and when they are open. Unfortunately, opening and closing hours change from year to year. And natives—even generally well-informed ones—may not bc rcliable about this kind of information. Local residents tend not to go to museums in their own city very often, so their advice may not be as helpful as one would expect. That goes even for the hotel staff one ordinarily counts on to know such things. In Italy there are museums that open their doors at 9 A.M., 10 A.M., 4 P.M., and Lord knows what other times. Some close at 1 P.M., some at 2 P.M., some at 7 P.M. They are

Hubert and Jan van Eyck
The Ghent Altarpiece
(closed, detail).
Completed 1432.
Oil on panel, 11′3″ x 14′5″.
St. Bavo, Ghent, Belgium

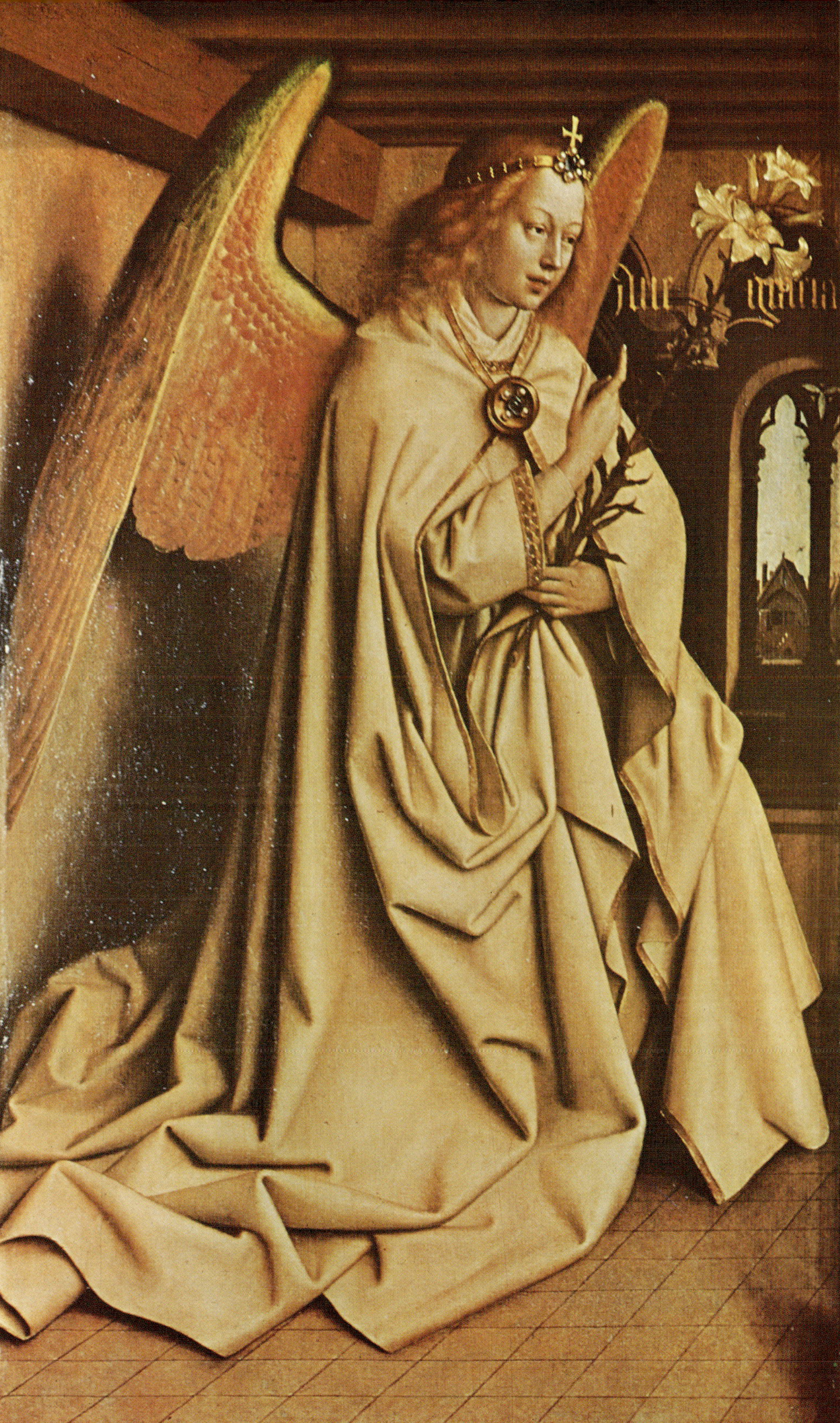

usually closed on Mondays, but some are open only three days a week or even one day, and some even for just a couple of hours. Also, summer and winter schedules may differ. There are guidebooks that give reasonably up-to-date information on opening hours, but the only way to be absolutely sure is to check with the museums directly, either by going there or by asking the concierge (hall porter) to call them on the telephone.

If there are a half-dozen or more major museums, as there are, for instance, in Rome, how does one make a sensible selection? The Blue Guide to Rome states, "If time permits, at least three weeks should be devoted to Rome and its environs, though much will have to be missed. Those who can stay only a few days may obtain glimpses of its treasures by going on conducted sightseeing tours of the city and its environs." This may be good advice for general tourists, but not much help where seeing museums is concerned.

The Blue Guide outlines its recommendations for twenty-one days of intensive sightseeing. In the October 1983 issue of *Connoisseur* magazine, Thomas Hoving gives his recipe for "7½ Glorious Days in Rome," which on one day includes three museums, a church, and an art gallery. He has great cultural stamina, but most people's minds would be mush after a day like that. A more serious problem is that when most people go to Rome for the first time they have neither twenty-one days nor even seven and one-half.

What do you do if you have only two or three days? Much depends on how high museums are on your agenda for that trip. The first time my wife and I went to Italy we spent three or four days each in

Overleaf:
Matthias Grünewald
The Isenheim Altarpiece
(open): *The Annunciation; Virgin and Child with Angels; The Resurrection.*
c. 1511–12.
Tempera on panel,
wings: 8′10″ x 4′8″;
central scene:
8′10″ x 11′2½″.
Musée Unterlinden,
Colmar, France

Right: Detail

Rome, Florence, and Venice, which I think is what most people do on their initial visit. We certainly could not see everything, but it was a wonderfully rich introduction. We have been back many times over the years, and each time we see not only old museum friends but we discover masterpieces we never saw before.

PILGRIMAGES TO DISTANT LANDS. If you are especially devoted to the work of a particular artist, or a particular period of art, it can be a great advantage to make a special trip to a distant city just to see one masterpiece. It is worth traveling halfway around the world to see the *Isenheim Altarpiece* by Matthias Grunewald—one of the greatest works of all time—in the Unterlinden Museum in Colmar, France. The same is true of the altarpiece by Jan van

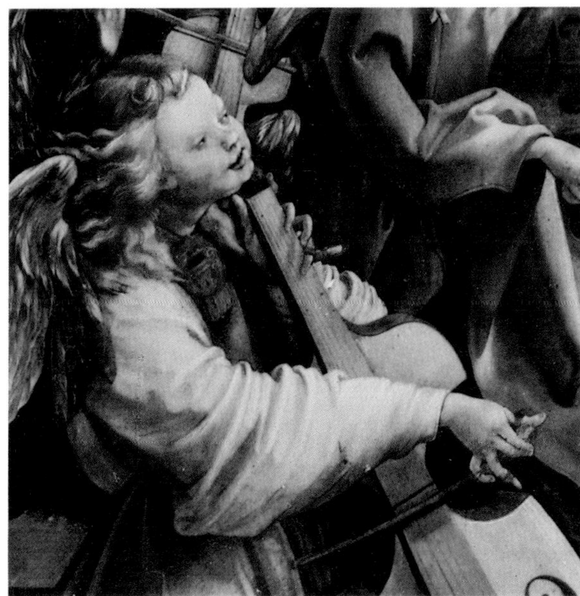

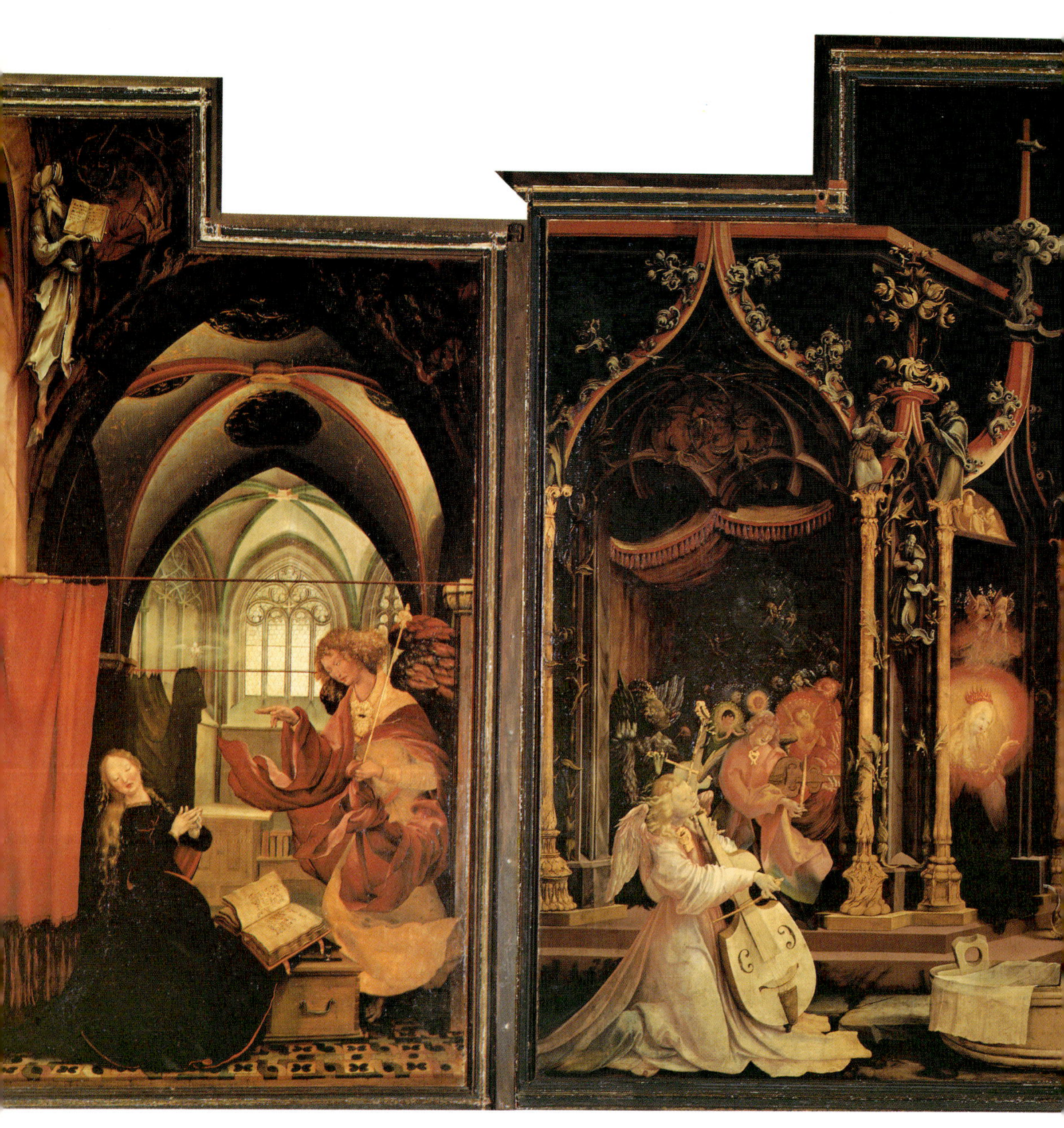

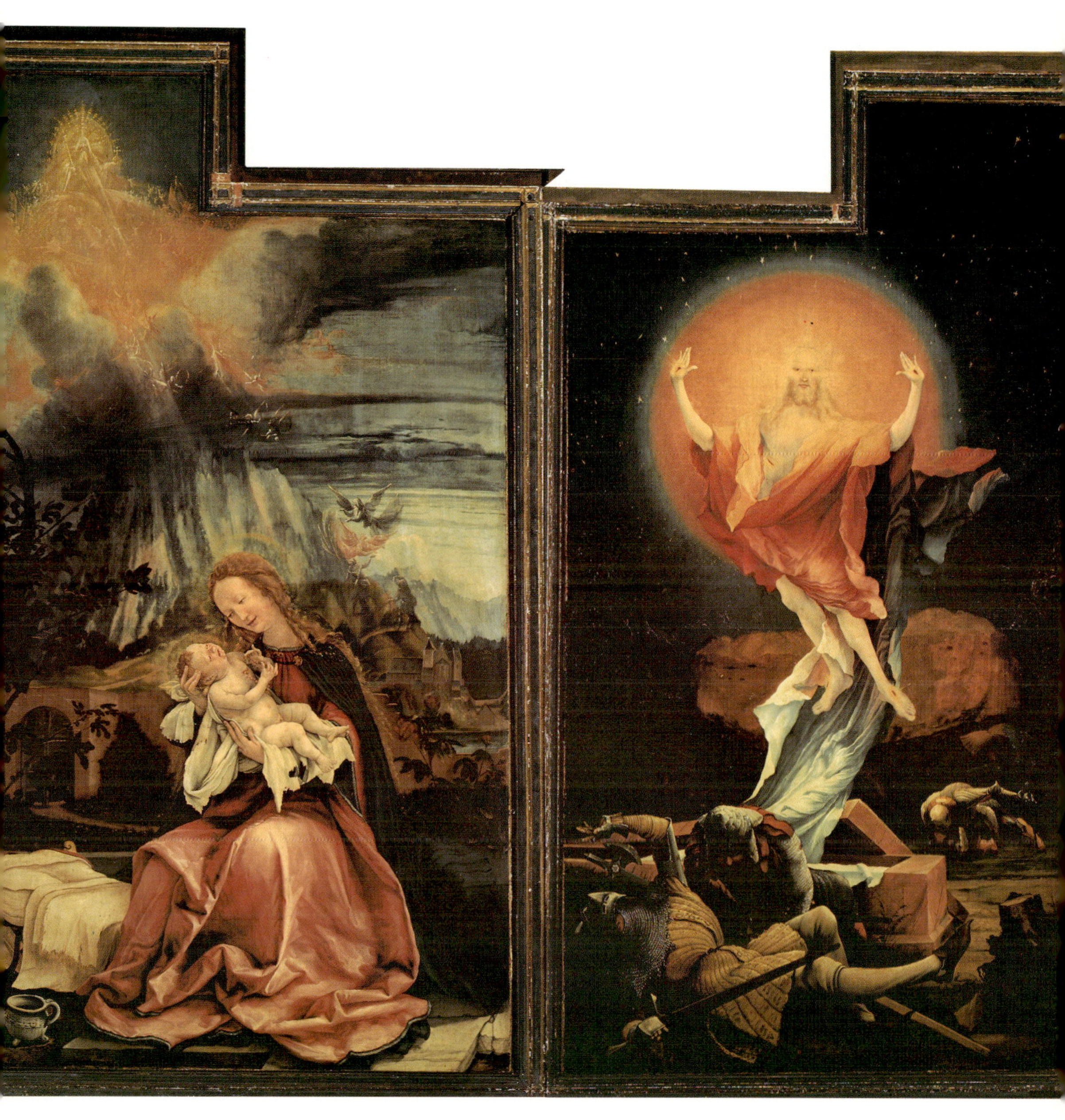

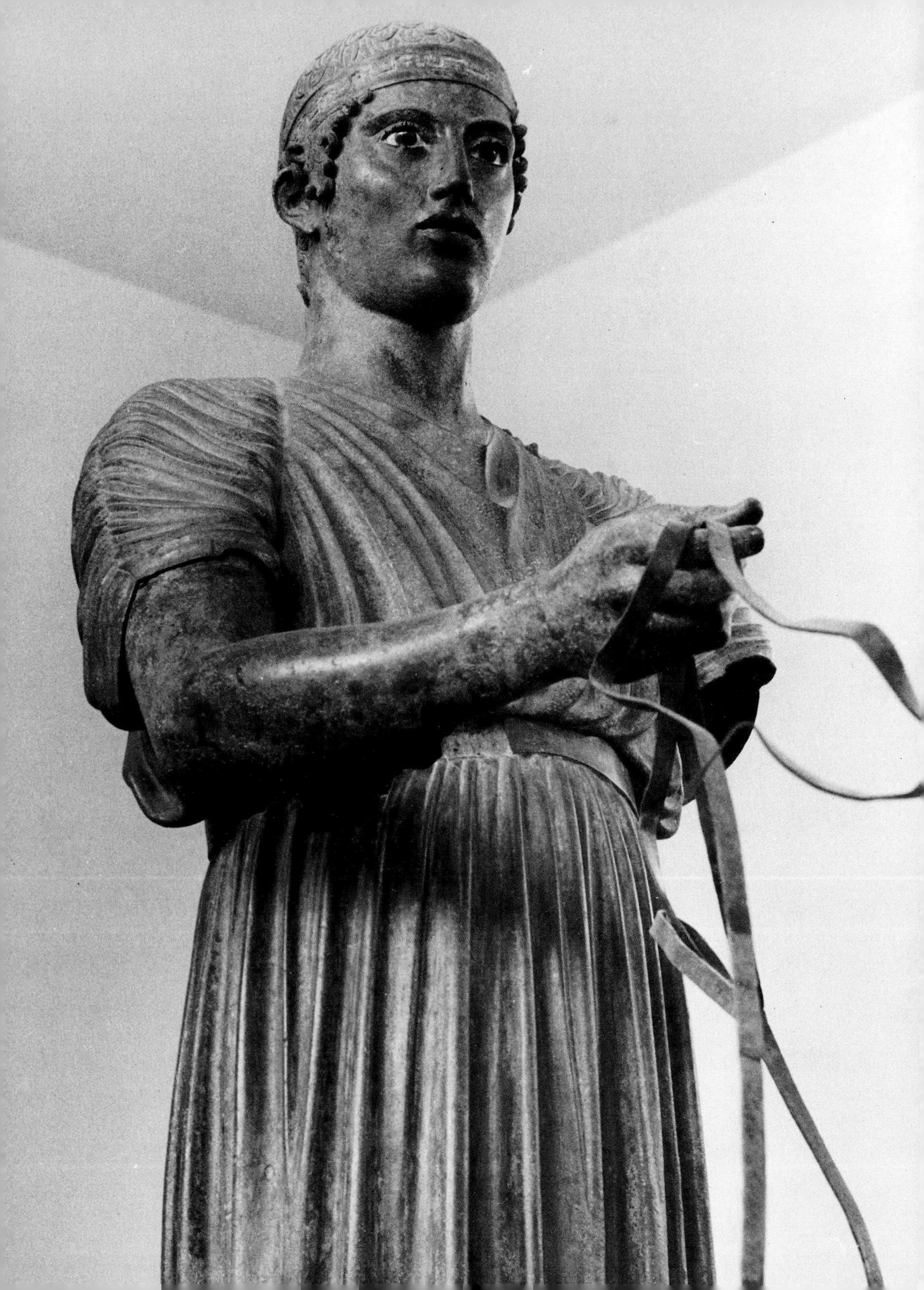

Opposite:
Charioteer of Delphi, from the Sanctuary of Apollo at Delphi (portion)
c. 470 B.C. Bronze, height 71″.
Archaeological Museum, Delphi

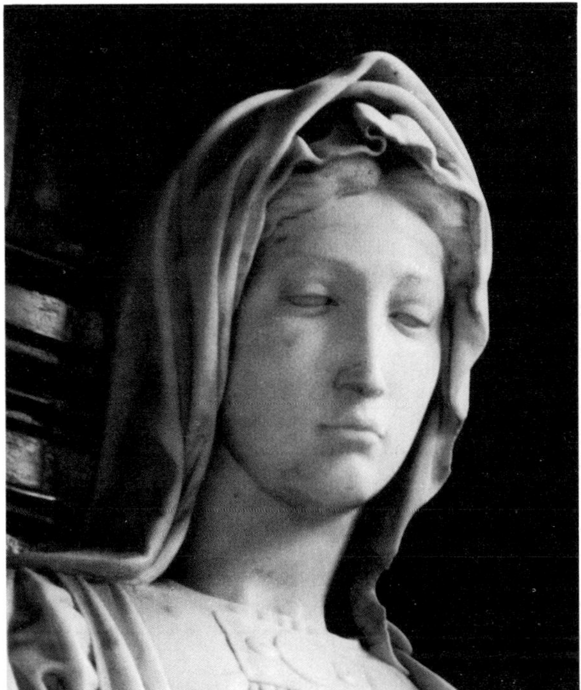

Michelangelo Buonarroti
The Bruges Madonna (detail).
c. 1503–4.
Marble; height (with base) 48″.
Onze Lieve Vrouwkerk, Bruges, Belgium

Eyck in Ghent, Belgium—and while there, one can go to nearby Bruges to see the Michelangelo *Madonna and Child* and Hans Memling's *Shrine of Saint Ursula*. A trip to Delphi, in Greece, to see *The Charioteer* and walk around the temple site is a unique experience.

One of the most memorable pilgrimages I ever made had to do with *The Madonna in Her Chamber* by Jan van Eyck, which was reproduced in *Life* magazine when I was about sixteen years old. There was something about that painting that I found incredibly beautiful, and I literally fell in love with it. I cut out the reproduction and mounted it on the inside door of my bedroom closet, where I looked at it every morning for years. The *Life* article stated that it was in the National Gallery of Victoria in Melbourne, Aus-

Overleaf:
After Jan van Eyck
The Madonna and Child.
1433.
Oil on panel, 10⅜ x 7⅝″.
The National Gallery of Victoria, Melbourne.
Felton Bequest, 1922

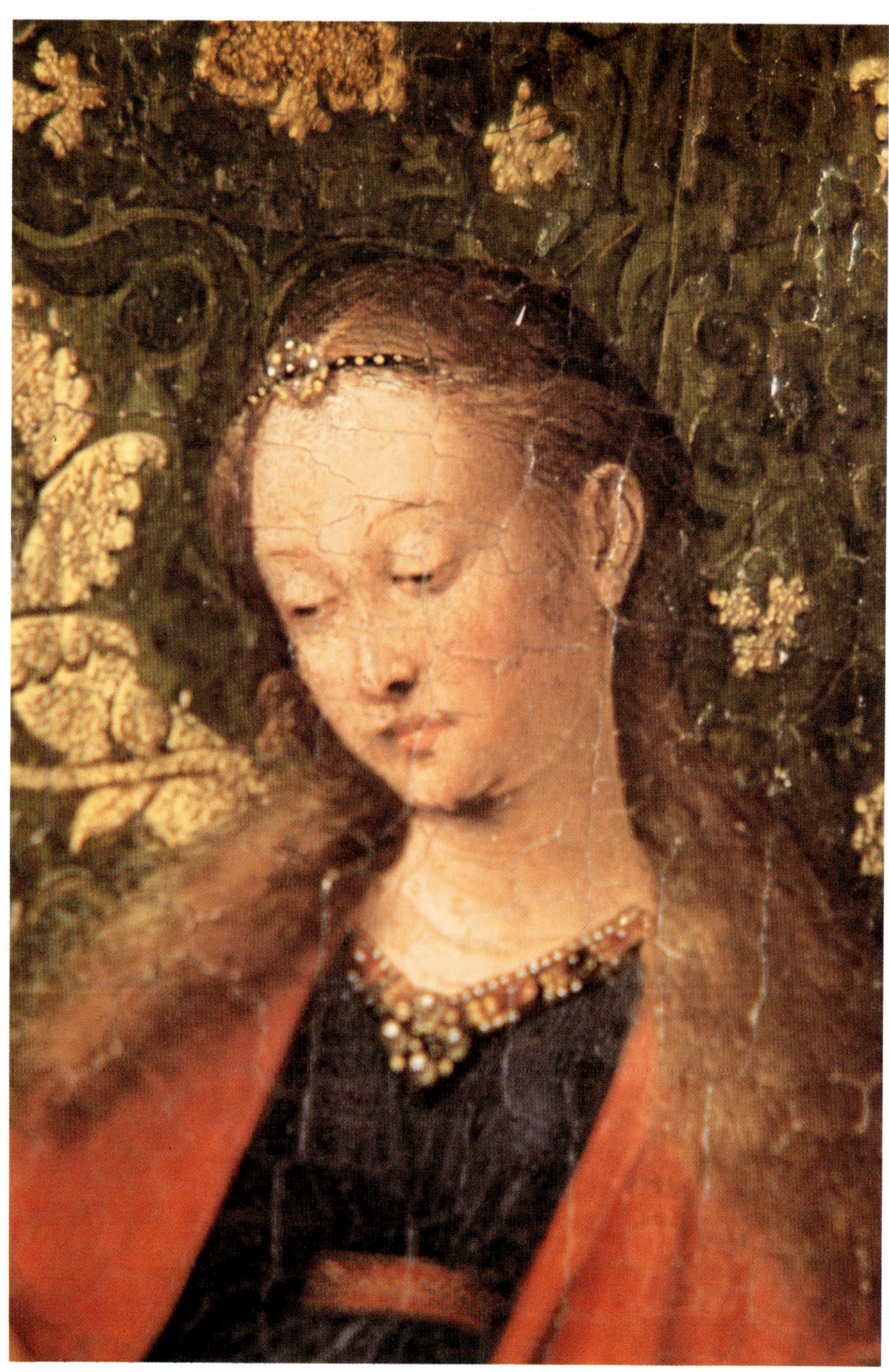

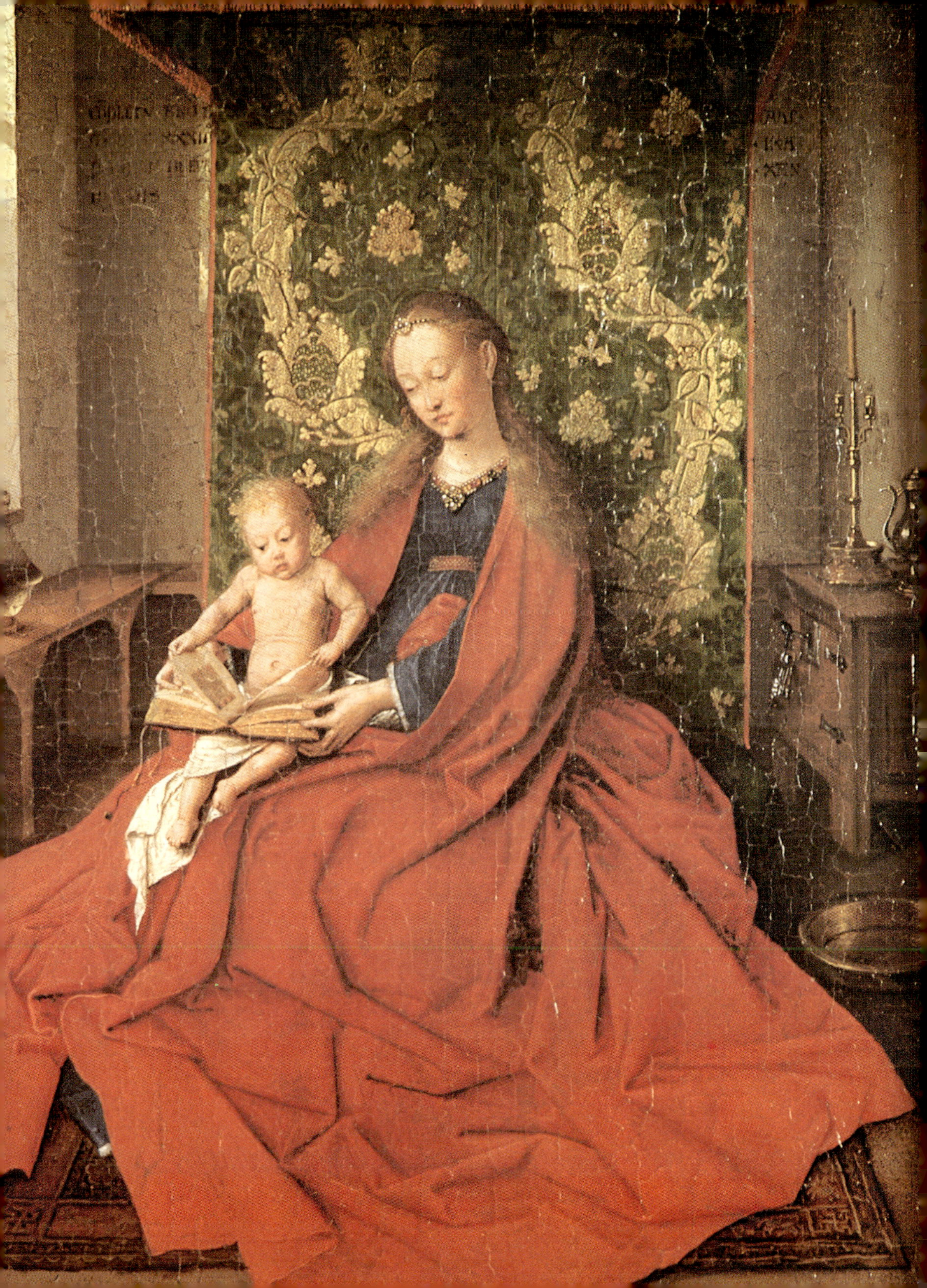

tralia, and I once wrote the director asking if there was a large reproduction of the painting I could buy. Unfortunately, I never received a reply. I did not realize at the time that it was a very small painting and that the *Life* reproduction was virtually life-size. My dream was to see the painting itself some day.

About thirty-five years later the opportunity to visit Melbourne finally arrived. This time I wrote to the museum in advance and asked for permission to photograph the painting. When I arrived at the museum, I discovered to my delight that the director had arranged to take the painting to his own office for me, and I was able to spend as much time as I wanted to study it minutely and photograph all the details to my heart's content. The painting is now only "attributed" to Van Eyck by some scholars, but it is good to remember Beethoven's comment about a piece attributed to Mozart: "If it is *not* by Mozart," he said, "it was written by someone who was a Mozart."

FAVORITE SUBJECTS. Besides the individual paintings that happen to be our favorites, there are different categories of subject matter that happen to catch our fancy. Some people are attracted to paintings of flowers, others to landscapes or seascapes, some to religious or historical works.

My special favorite is beautiful paintings and sculptures of nudes, and as I walk through a museum my eye picks out representations of nudes that are particularly striking. Early in life I was mesmerized by the Titians in the Uffizi in Florence, the Giorgiones in the Accademia in Venice and in the Louvre, the

Renoirs in the Barnes Foundation in Merion Station, Pennsylvania, the Correggios in the Galleria Borghese in Rome and in the National Gallery in London. But as time went on I enjoyed discovering nudes that were less well known and were in a way my personal acquisitions. There was, for instance, the magnificent Furini *St. Lucy* in the Galleria Spada in Rome, the superb nudes in the Henner Museum in Paris, the wonderful nudes by Boucher in the Wallace Collection in London, and what may well be Boucher's greatest masterpiece in the Norton Simon Museum in Pasadena.

The secret of finding those treasures that speak most directly to you is keeping your mind and eyes open to appealing forms as you walk through a museum. One of the most beautiful objects in the British Museum is a spectacular life-size, gilt-bronze female figure called *The Bodhisattva Tara.* A twelfth-century sculpture from Sri Lanka, it is exhibited in a display case that could easily be missed by a visitor walking quickly through the gallery. When I first started thinking about writing *How to Visit a Museum,* I took a series of photographs of that particular sculpture, showing how one would first notice it in its display case and then how one would come closer to examine its extraordinary details—the proud head; the rich, full breasts; the slender waist and undulating hips; the graceful position of the arms. I would have missed something very rewarding in my life had I never seen this sculpture.

Of course, there are some nudes I do not like, and you may or may not react as I do to paintings and sculptures of nudes. The point is seek out the subject matter that has special appeal for *you*.

Overleaf left:
The Bodhisattva Tara
Sinhalese, c. 10th century.
Bronze and gilt, height 4′9″.
British Museum, London

Overleaf right:
Guido Reni
Atalanta and Hippomenes
(detail). 1625.
Oil on panel, 6′3¼″ x 8′7⅞″.
Museo di Capodimonte,
Naples

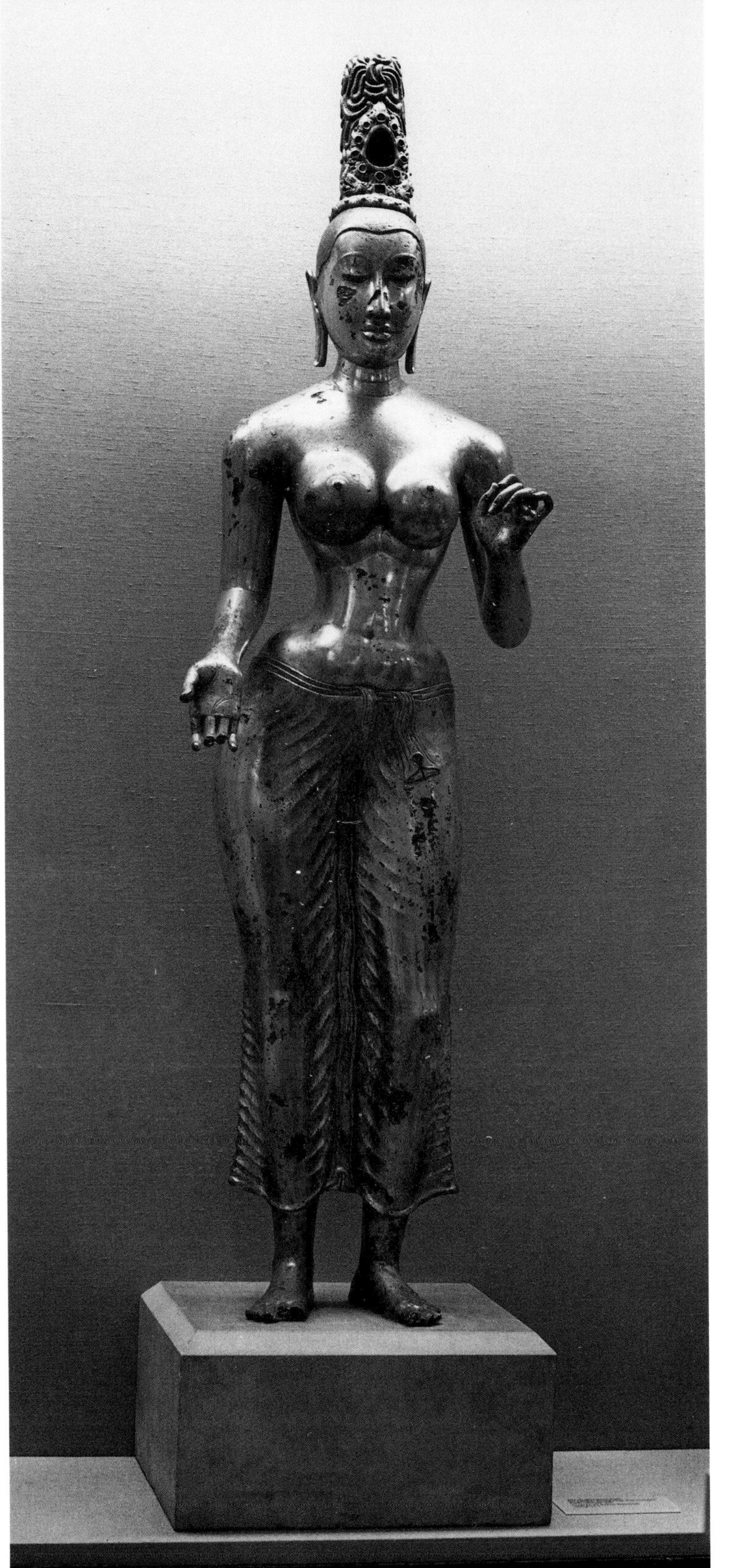

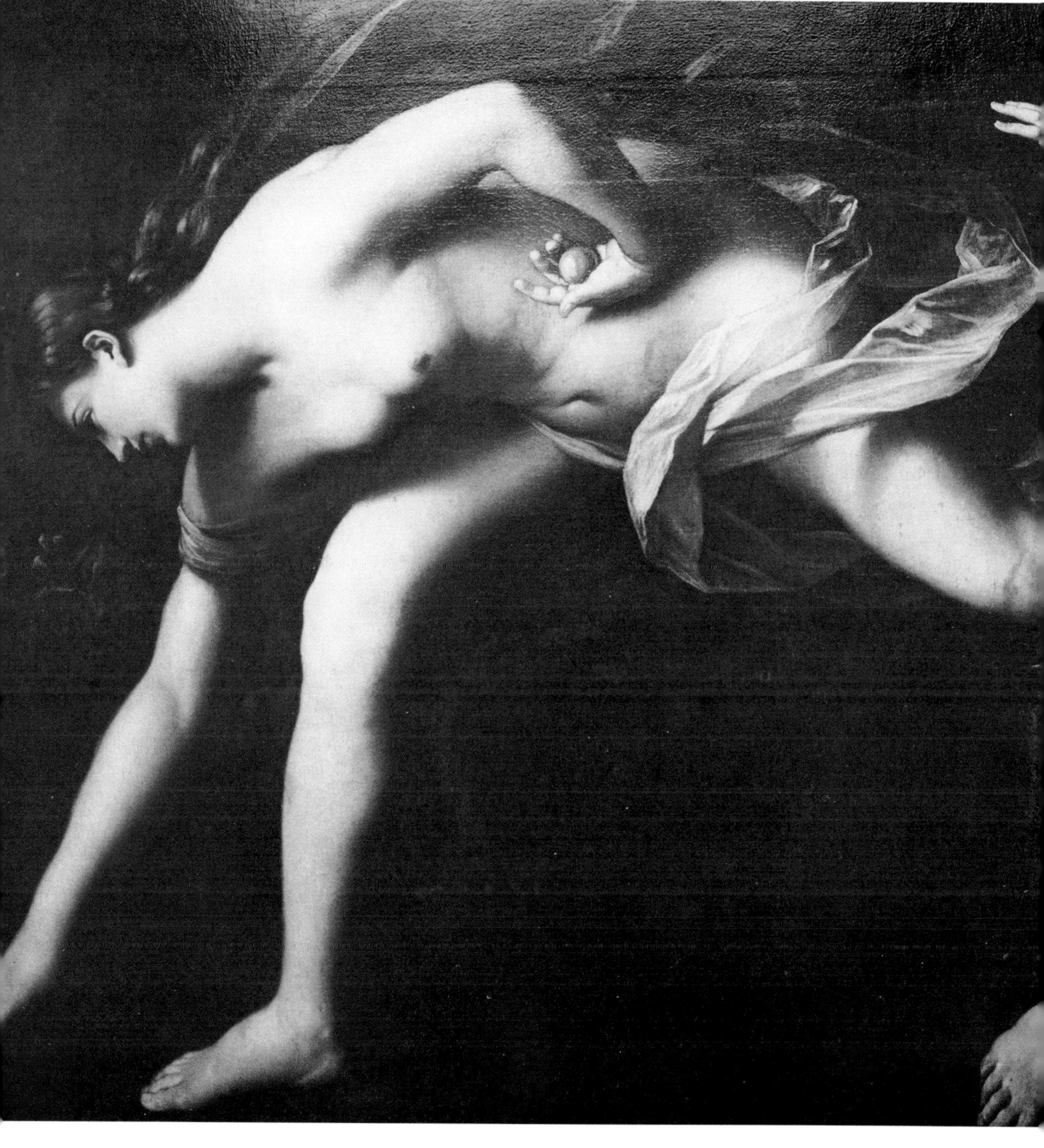

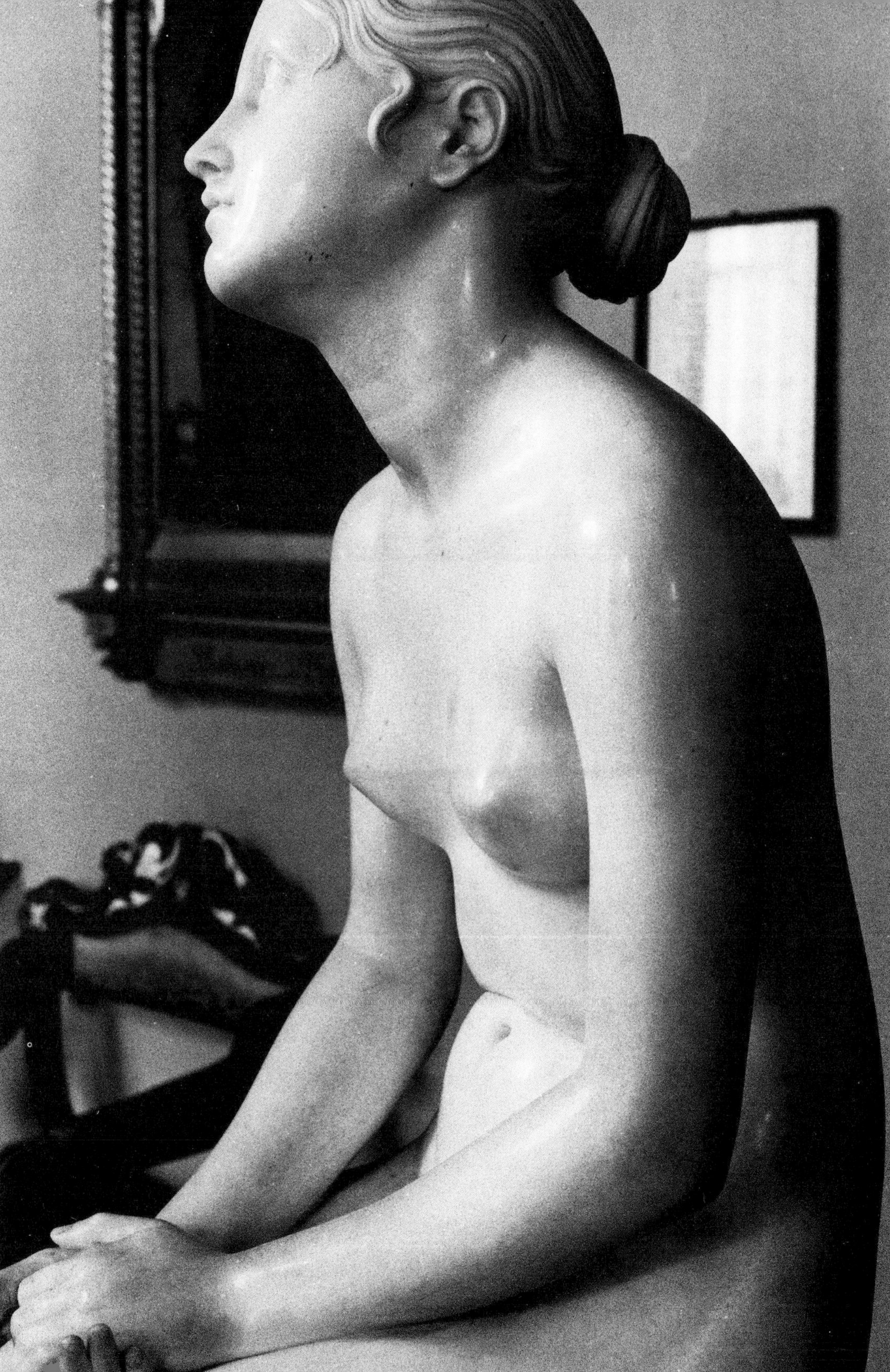

Lorenzo Bartolino
Trust in God. 1835.
Marble, life-size.
Poldi-Pezzoli Museum,
Milan

LEARNING AS YOU GO. When you do come across a work that makes an enduring imprint on your esthetic consciousness, note the name of the artist for future reference. I discovered the name of the nineteenth-century sculptor Giovanni Dupré because I fell in love with a beautiful seminude figure in the Church of San Lorenzo in Florence which I happened to come across almost by accident. Subsequently I discovered another extraordinary Dupré figure in the Norton Simon Museum in Pasadena, another in the National Gallery of Modern Art in Rome, and two more in the Gallery of Modern Art in Florence, and five in, of all places, a hotel named Mona Lisa in Florence, which I came across quite by accident and which is owned by the Dupré family. Now I have my eye out for Dupré sculpture wherever I go.

The same thing happened to me in Milan when I discovered a beautiful nude painting by Francesco Hayez, *Odalisca,* in the Pinacoteca di Brera and a lovely kneeling figure by Lorenzo Bartolini in the Poldi Pezzoli Museum. Both "finds" set me off on further searches for the work of those artists. When I saw an exhibition of paintings by William-Adolphe Bouguereau at the New York Cultural Center, I found his nude figures so wonderfully sensuous that I could understand for the first time why Renoir and many of his contemporaries considered him the leading artist of his time. And when I came across *A Summer Night* by Albert Moore at the Walker Art Gallery in Liverpool, I had my first taste of those beautiful nudes with which the Victorian painters and sculptors entertained their otherwise prudish audiences. Once you discover artists whose work have a special meaning

Overleaf left:
François Boucher
Vertumnus and Pomona.
c. 1740–45.
Oil on canvas, 62¾ x 66⅜".
The Norton Simon Museum,
Pasadena, California

Overleaf right:
Titian
Flora. c. 1516–20.
Oil on canvas, 31⅛ x 24⅞".
Galleria degli Uffizi,
Florence

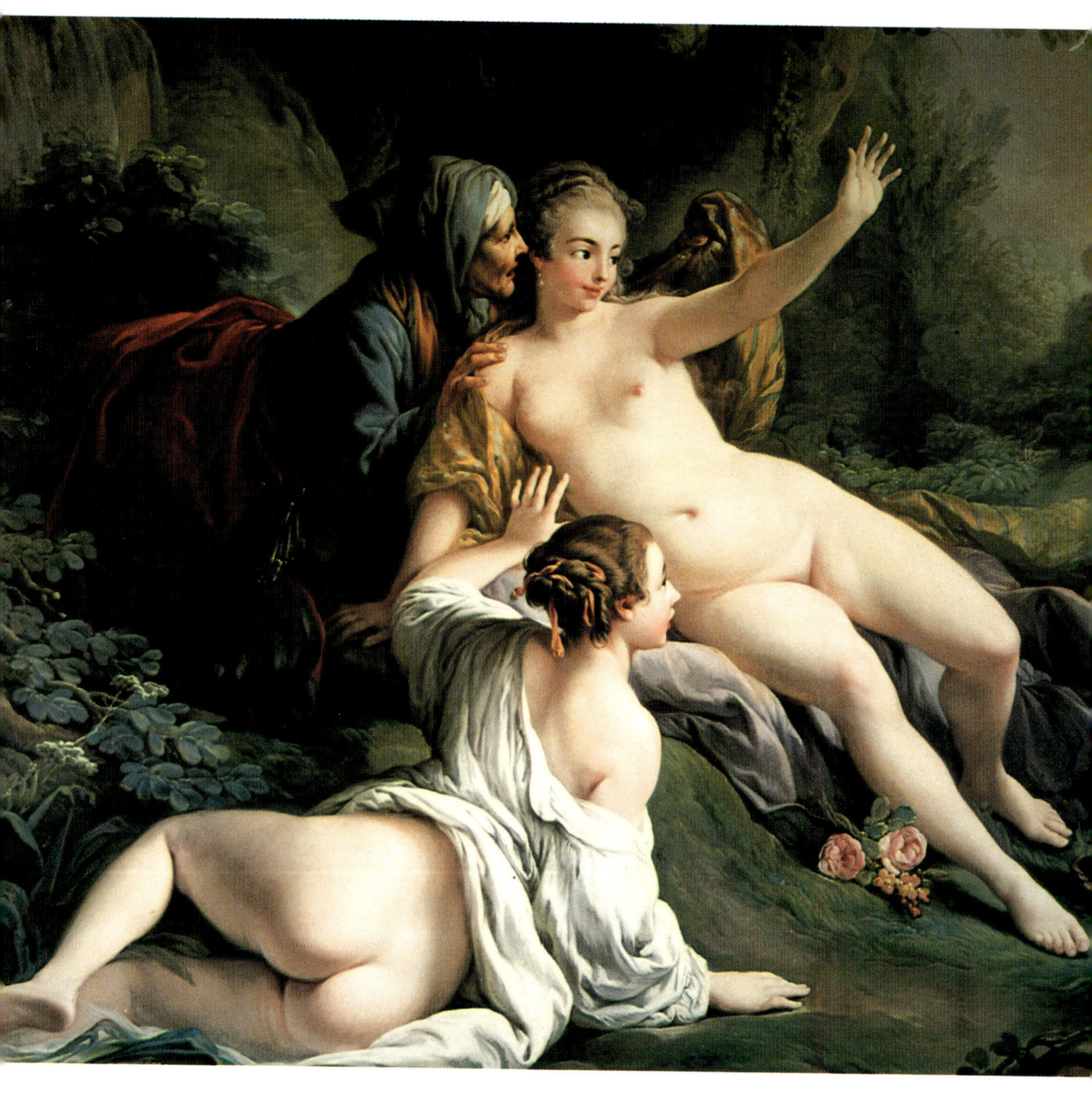

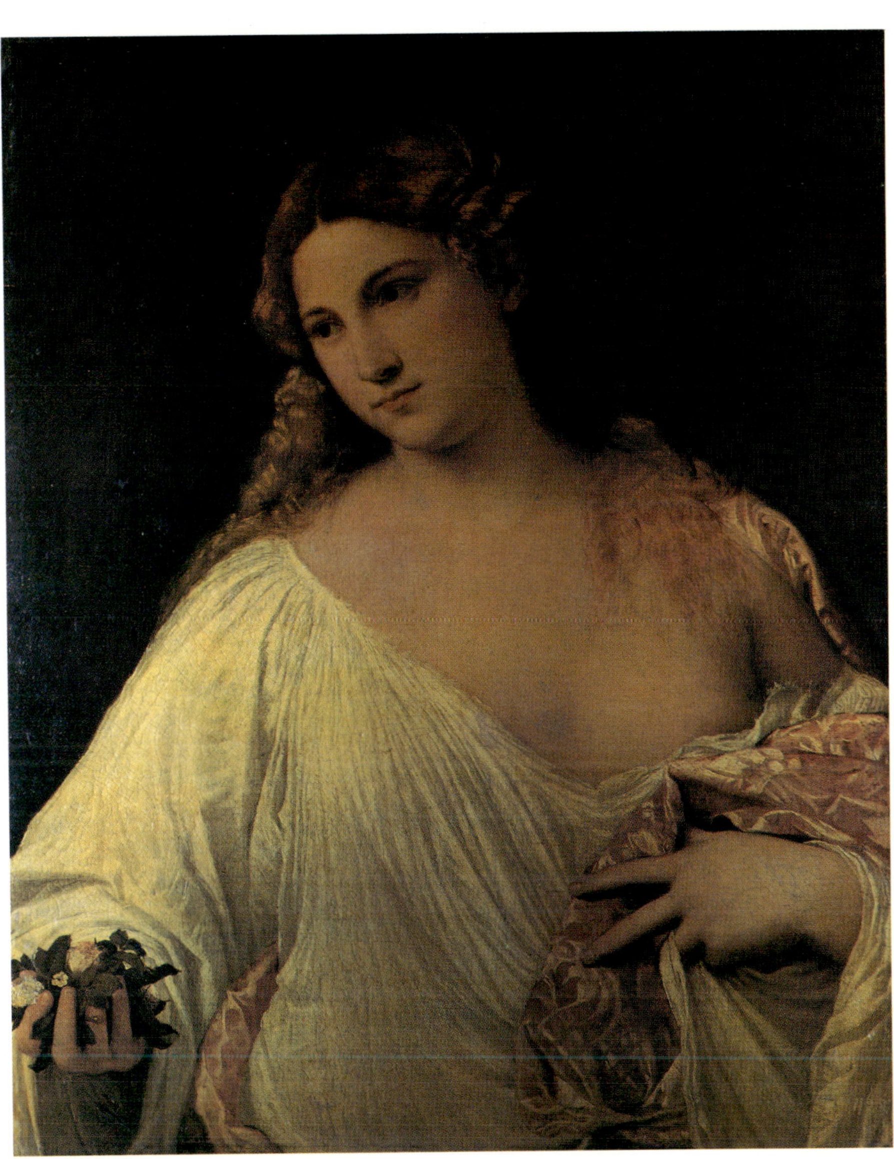

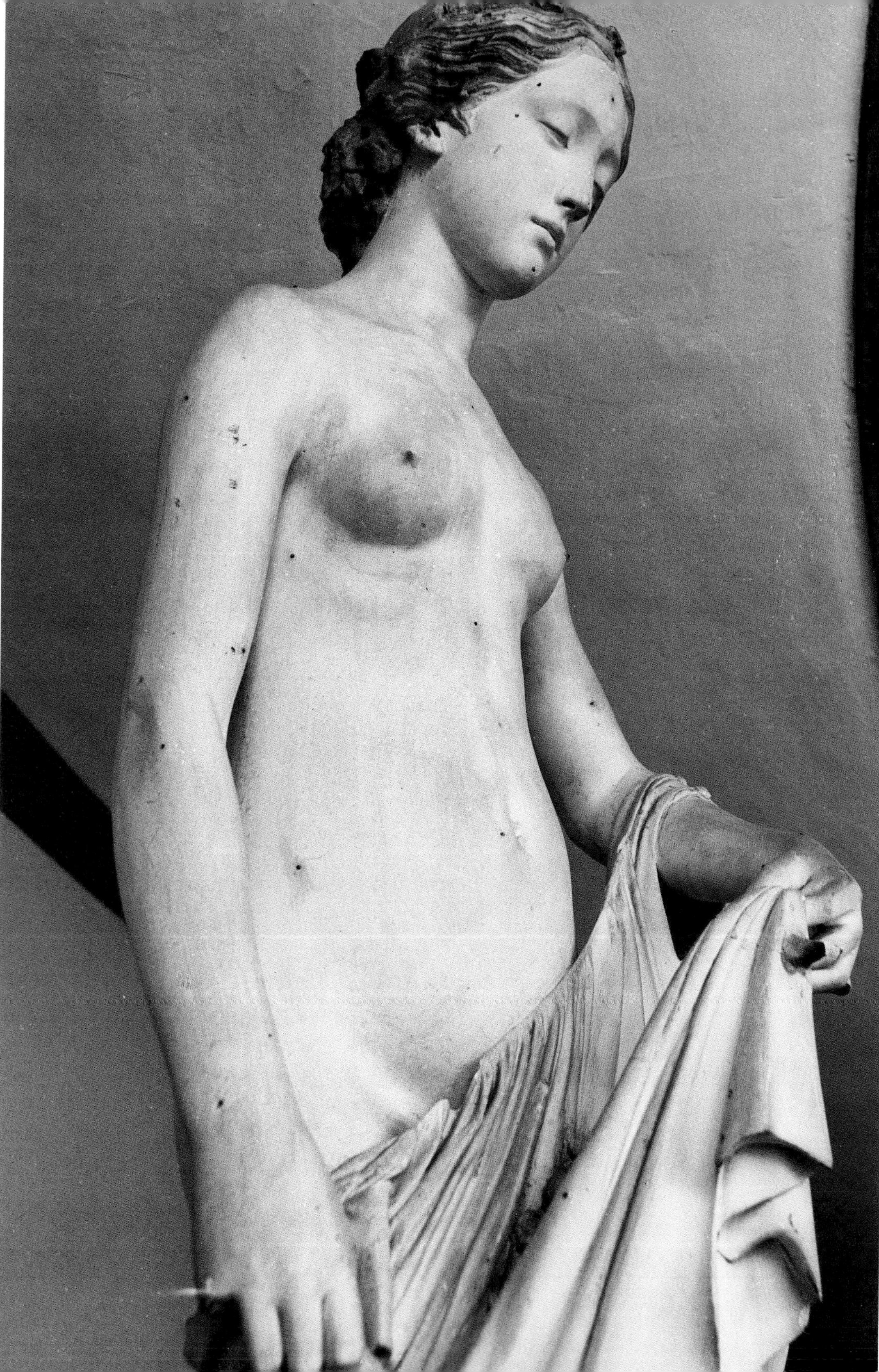

Giovanni Dupré
Mona Lisa.
Plaster, life-size. Mona Lisa Hotel, Florence

for you, you can look for other paintings or sculptures by them in different museums.

Whenever you can, you should plan to steal an hour or so in any city you visit anywhere in the world for a quick look at the local museum. Even when you are traveling to a meeting and have one or two business associates with you, drag them along to the major art museum in town. They may be startled by the idea of taking time out from work to "get a little culture," but they will probably enjoy it.

SPECIAL EXHIBITIONS. In recent years, as museums have proliferated at an unbelievable rate around the world, another phenomenon has been growing in popularity—the special exhibition that brings treasures from far away to produce a one-time-only cultural experience. These special exhibitions take various forms. They may consist of masterpieces from one museum such as the Hermitage, the Mauritshuis, the Louvre, or the Vatican. They may be on a particular theme like "Post-Impressionists" or "Tutankhamen." They may be collected works of a single artist like El Greco, Manet, Picasso, or Henry Moore.

One cannot help wondering whether the enormous crowds attracted by some of these "blockbuster" exhibitions are more impressed by the celebrity of the objects than by their artistic worth. Probably all of us experience a degree of both feelings, and certainly there is no doubt that when a group of objects is gathered together in a highly publicized show, there is a special sense of excitement about the event itself. The designers of the exhibition create a museum drama in the presentation

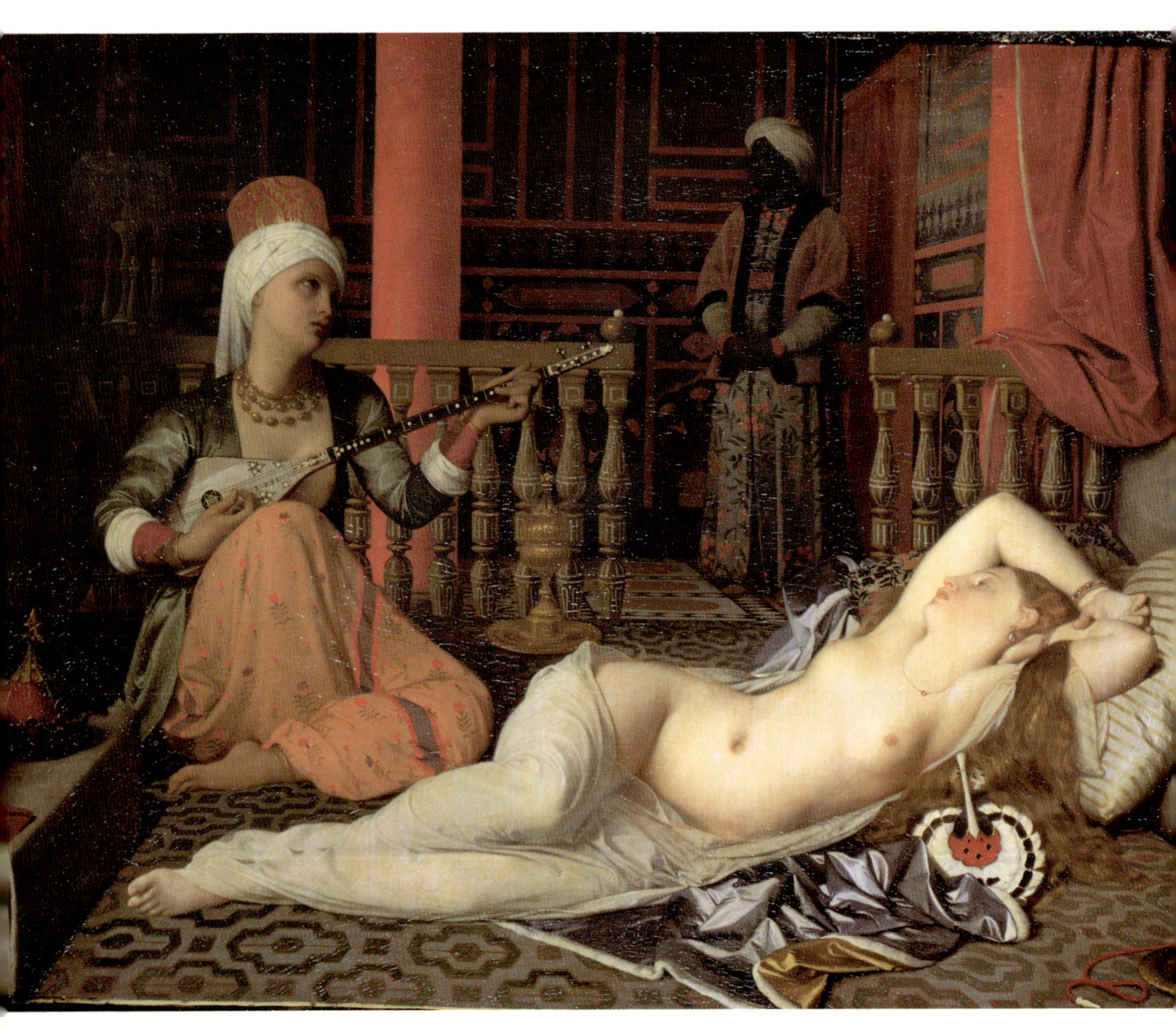

Jean-Auguste-Dominique Ingres
Odalisque with Slave. 1840.
Oil on canvas mounted on panel, 28⅜ x 39⅜".
Fogg Art Museum, Harvard University, Cambridge, Massachusetts.
Bequest of Grenville L. Winthrop

of the works. This includes special lighting, careful placement of the works, even the shape of the rooms and exhibition spaces. The resulting overall impression may be more enduring than if one had seen the objects in their original museum locations.

One problem about seeing a much-heralded special exhibition is that impressions are created in your mind before you ever reach the museum. One should recognize that a review by an art critic represents only one expert opinion, with which you may disagree. Art critics do not have the same life-or-death power as theater critics, but they generate word-of-mouth talk that may predispose you to like or dislike what you are going to see. You should always be prepared to decide for yourself whether you agree with what you have heard or read.

Still another potential problem is caused by the emphasis given to certain key works reproduced in a catalogue. These are, presumably, the curator's or editor's choice, but this does not mean that you should not make up your own mind about what is outstanding. You can make personal discoveries in special exhibitions by keeping your eye open for what appeals to *you*, whether or not it is highlighted in the exhibition or featured in the catalogue.

It is a great treat to have works brought together that one might not otherwise be able to see, but there is nothing wrong with breezing through the exhibition to see if anything catches your eye or heart. You may want to linger here or there, or even come back to savor some of the works you especially enjoyed. If you find little to attract your interest, you may walk through the galleries in a matter of minutes, and conclude that this one was not for you.

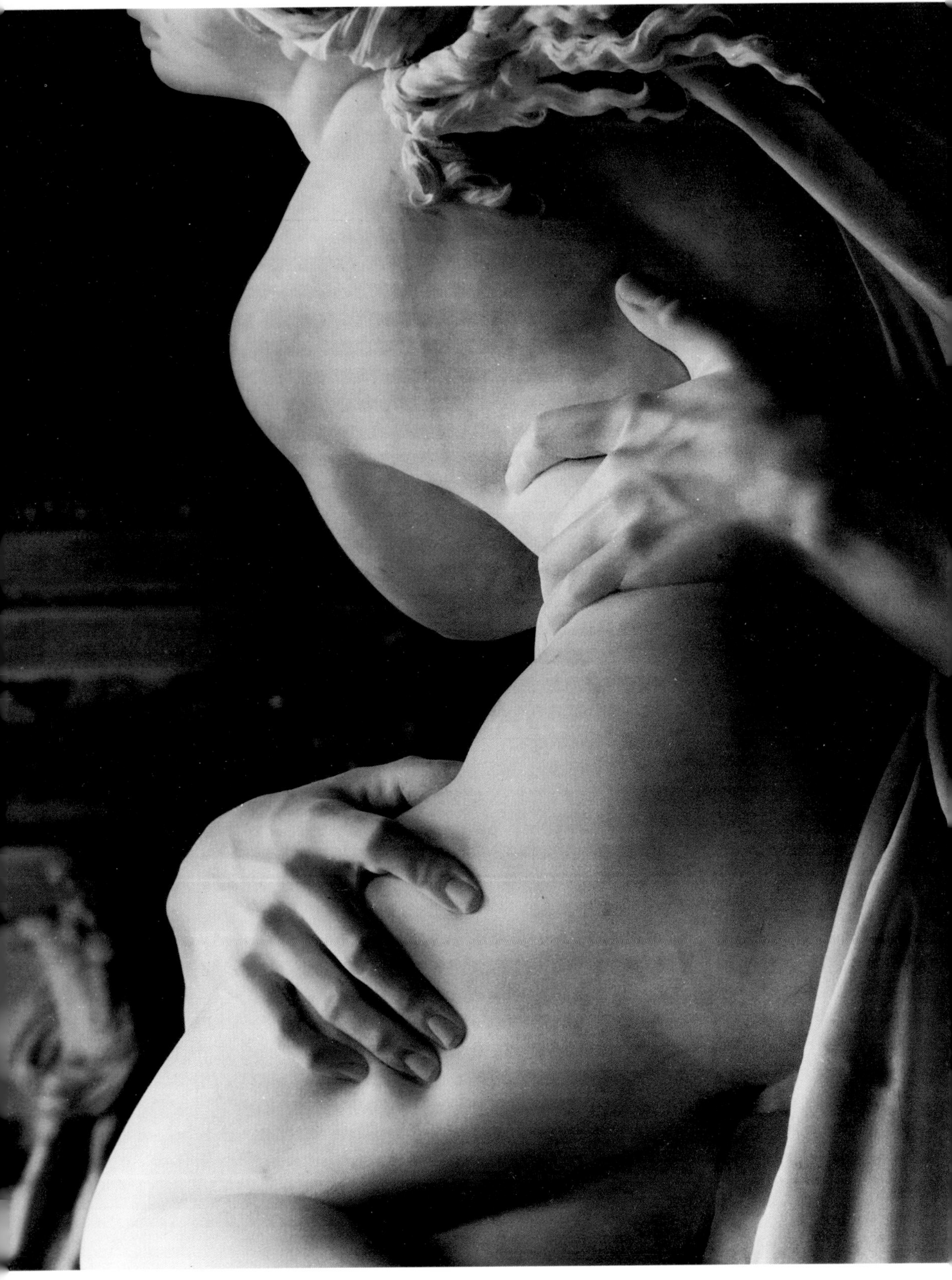

Gian Lorenzo Bernini
Pluto and Proserpina
(detail). 1621–22.
Marble, over life-size.
Galleria Borghese, Rome

One of the unfortunate consequences of the increasing popularity of special exhibitions is the decreasing attention visitors pay to permanent collections. I was particularly struck by this phenomenon at the Vatican exhibition. After going through it at the Metropolitan Museum, I walked across the second floor to meet someone at the other end of the building. On the way I passed through galleries in which there were cases after cases of Greek vases. There had been one small room in the Vatican exhibition devoted to a handful of such vases, and crowds had stopped in awe to admire them. But there was not a soul in the galleries just down the hall with perhaps ten times as many vases of equal quality!

Try to make a point of visiting some part of the permanent collection of a museum whenever you go to see a special exhibition. You can continue to discover new wonders in sections of the museum that you have missed in the past. You can never walk through a gallery of a great museum and not discover something new and marvelous that has escaped your attention in the past.

EXHIBITION HALLS. There are, of course, many institutions devoted only to special exhibitions; these have few if any works of art in their permanent collections. The Royal Academy of Arts in London and the Grand Palais in Paris are outstanding examples of such institutions, and they provided a model for the special exhibition galleries like the Arthur Sackler Wing of the Metropolitan Museum. In these galleries, one always looks to see "what's on" when one visits a city, just as one would check theater, ballet, opera, or concert halls.

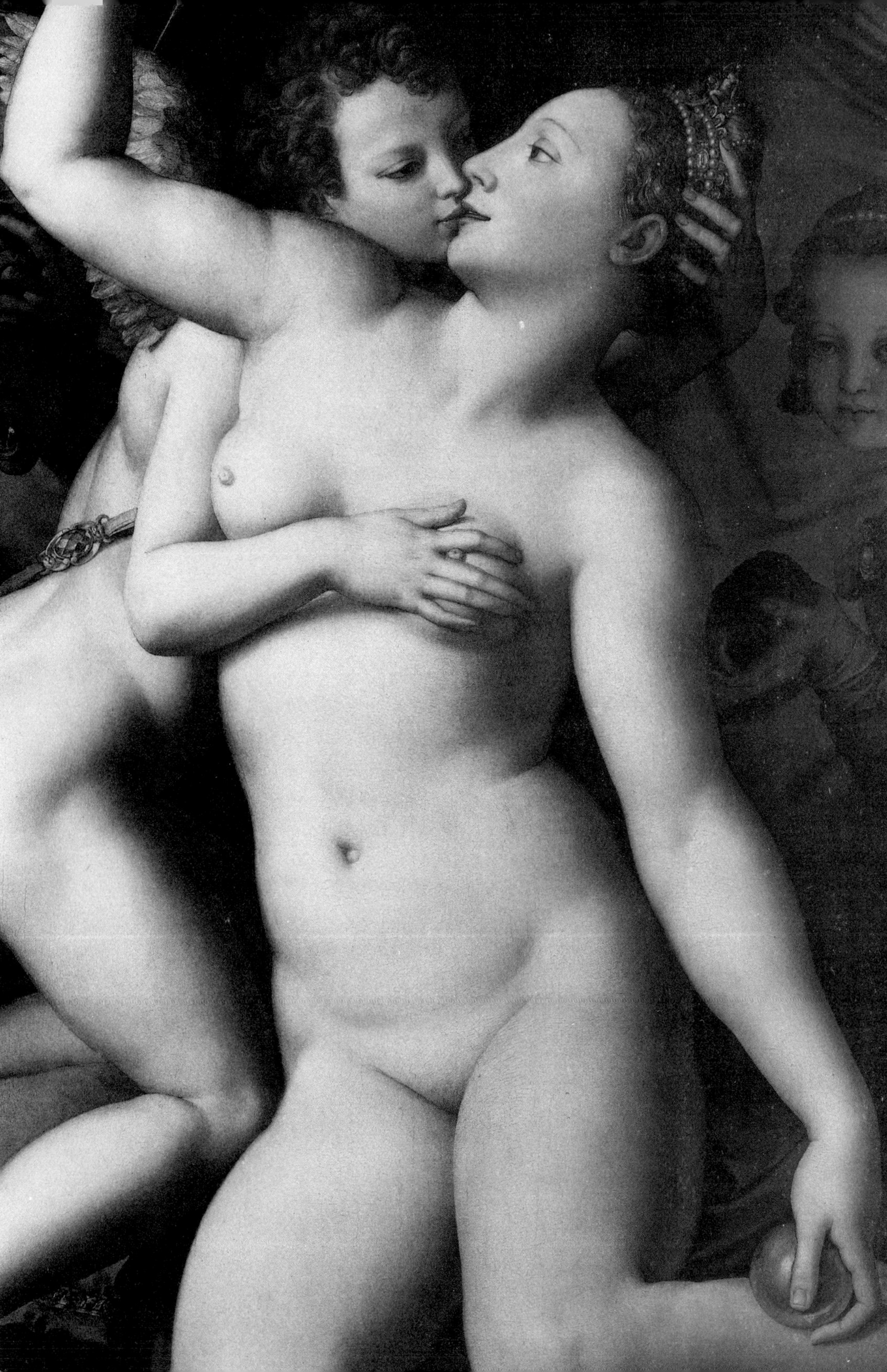

Angelo Bronzino
An Allegory of Time and Love. 1546.
Oil on panel, 61 x 56¾″.
National Gallery, London

Even in these exhibition halls, however, it is worth keeping your eyes open for unexpected discoveries among works of art you might otherwise take for granted. After visiting the Royal Academy in London for years to see special exhibitions, one day I noticed paintings hung over the staircase on the way to the galleries. They were outstanding works by the Italian Mannerist Sebastiano Ricci. I do not know how many times I had passed those two paintings without looking at them, but I suspect I never will do so again.

Then, too, if you keep an open mind you may find yourself introduced to new and surprising experiences. A few years ago there was an exhibition of contemporary art in London's Tate Gallery which included a work by Carl Andre consisting of a long line of bricks laid out across the floor. There was an uproar in the press about what many observers felt was a hoax, but the creators of the exhibition stood fast in their conviction that the work was a legitimate statement having to do with the delineation of space, the use of familiar materials that are taken for granted, the floor as an area of a room that can be as much of a setting for creative ideas as any other area, and so forth. Because of the controversy, people flocked to the exhibition. For the most part they looked at the string of bricks in disbelief, but they did look, and the synapses of their brains were probably exercised a bit by what they saw.

MUSEUMS IN YOUR OWN CITY. There seems to be a peculiar block in many people's minds against going back to museums in one's own city to see works in permanent collections. Since they will be there tomorrow, it does not seem worth a trip to see them today. Even while passing through a gallery in which familiar works are on display, one tends to give them short shrift because they are familiar, and this is even more of a problem if the works have been reproduced extensively in postcards or posters and become an artistic commonplace.

One good way to overcome this mental block is to find reasons to visit museums in your home town. Attending lectures is one good way to accomplish this. Going with an out-of-town visitor is another. Having lunch in the museum cafeteria with a friend is still another way to get in the mood to spend a few moments in permanent collections. Or one can try to get into the habit of taking time out on a regular basis to go to local museums.

The truth is that one can never see a major work of art too often. There is always something new to enjoy in it. Indeed, that may be the definition of a great work of art—its unlimited power to excite one's esthetic sensibilities.

A LIFELONG ADVENTURE. You are not likely to remember the names of artists whose works have especially appealed to you, or where you saw a particular painting or sculpture, unless you make a special effort to keep track. One purpose in spending a few moments in the museum shop after your visit is over is to find some memento that will help preserve your experiences. Postcard reproductions (or larger ones that can be mounted or framed) of your favorite works will certainly help. So will catalogues of the museum collections or of the work of individual artists you particularly enjoyed on this visit.

If you follow this practice, museum-going will

become a cumulative experience rather than a one-shot affair. It will be a lifelong adventure during which you will accumulate your favorites as you visit new museums and revisit old ones. You will find new favorites as your taste changes. Your books and postcards and reproductions will be like a changing exhibition reflecting what is particularly exciting to you at any given moment. Your museum-at-home will be a personal expression of where your mind and heart is at this stage of your art enjoyment.

Some people think postcard reproductions are unsophisticated ways of enjoying works of art. The color may be wrong, the size out of scale, and the subtlety of the image missing. Yet something of the original work is represented in the reproduction that can be appreciated by the most knowledgeable art lover. Kenneth Clark had an extraordinary collection of drawings, prints, paintings, and sculpture by the masters in his apartment in London and his home in Saltwood, but he also had postcard reproductions on his mantlepiece of works that fit his current mood. In addition, he had recently acquired books piled up on tables where one could thumb through them. One had the feeling that the original works in his collection were a part of his life, but that new esthetic interests were continuously stimulated by a procession of reproductions and commentaries that reminded him of great works he had seen elsewhere.

A WAY OF LIFE. Museum visitors may range anywhere from the casually interested to the passionately devoted. If you are not even casually interested, my advice would be not to bother at all. Just going through the motions of visiting a museum and walking through the galleries is not likely to start the juices flowing. One chief executive officer of a major corporation told me that he has spent a good deal of time talking to guards in front of museums in different parts of the world while his wife visited inside. I respected him for his honesty, not only with me but with himself.

But if there is an ember of interest in your heart, try to fan it as best you can. Look at what appeals to you. Admit freely what does not. Build on what appeals to you. If something gets you excited, it may be the beginning of a whole new way of life. Try to remember names, places, dates as a reference for future museum visits. Take something home with you to keep the memory alive. Go to another museum when you can, even if it is the one around the corner that you have not set foot in since you were a child. Let yourself be surprised by something you like today that you never liked before. Commune with a work of art to see what you personally can find in it that is meaningful or moving, and talk to someone close to you about what makes a special impact. Listen to others talk about their feelings and see whether that helps you appreciate something that you could not see before.

Museums are there for *you*. They can give you something that only kings and queens had in days gone by, an opportunity to be with the greatest masterpieces of all time. If you know how to make the most of your museum-going adventures, you can even take some record of your favorite works home with you and make them a permanent part of your life.

Photographs are by David Finn, New York, with the exception of the following: A.C.L., Brussels, 107; ARXIU MAS, Barcelona, 11; British Museum, London, 15; F. Bruckmann, Munich, 109; Ludovico Canali, Rome, 123; Fogg Art Museum, Cambridge, Massachusetts, 126; The Frick Collection, New York, 72; Gabinetto Fotografico, Florence, 32; The Solomon R. Guggenheim Museum, New York, 81; Hirmer Verlag, Munich, 112; Kröller-Müller Foundation, Otterlo, 86; The Louvre, Paris, 42, 43, 60, 61; The Metropolitan Museum of Art, New York, 57, 92; The National Gallery, London, 2, 3, 20, 22–26, 46, 47, 66, 67, 130; National Gallery of Art, Washington, D.C., 90; Schwitter, Ltd., Basel, 110, 111; The Norton Simon Museum of Art, Pasadena, California, 123; Julius Shulman, Malibu, California, 79; Whitney Museum of American Art, New York, 62, 63.